ANDREW CAYMAN

OPTIONS TRADING

---

2 BOOKS IN 1:

Options Trading Crash Course + Options And Day
Trading. Start Investing In Otions, Stocks And
Futures Like An Expert Trader.

THIS BOOK INCLUDES

BOOK 1:

OPTIONS TRADING CRASH COURSE:

The Complete Crash Course To Investing And Making Money Online. Learn In 12 Days How To Trade Perfectly And Be Profitable On Stocks, Options, Futures.

BOOK 2:

OPTIONS AND DAY TRADING:

Everything You Need To Know To Make Money Online. Start Investing In Options, Stocks And Futures Like An Expert Trader.

© Copyright 2020 - All rights reserved.

ANDREW CAYMAN

OPTIONS TRADING

CRASH COURSE:

The Complete Crash Course To Investing And Making Money Online. Learn In 12 Days How To Trade Perfectly And Be Profitable On Stocks, Options, Futures.

Table of Contents

Introduction

Options trading is an extremely popular trading style for a wide range of investors. It tends to be utilized when investing in various financial instruments and options, such as futures, foreign currencies, and stocks. It's a style that is somewhere close to the specific short-term form of day trading and the longer-term approach of utilizing a buy and hold strategy.

It's typically a style utilized by those generally new to options trading, but at the same time, it's frequently supported by those who have higher experience also. There are various advantages to options trading and accurately, utilizing this style for trading options. Similarly, as with investment, there's a great deal of information you should learn before really beginning.

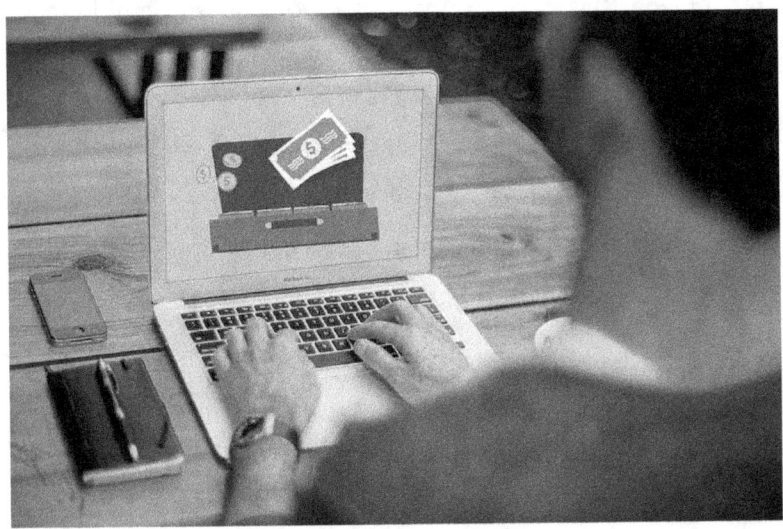

Options' trading is tied with searching for short-term price momentum and attempting to profit from that price force by buying and selling suitably. The value of options contracts is, to a great extent, dependent on the value of underlying securities. You are hoping to recognize the price energy of any financial instrument, such as stocks, and afterward trade the significant options contracts as indicated by how you anticipate that the hidden security will move.

You will enter a position and after that exiting it a short period later. That time can be anyplace between several days or half a month, contingent upon to what extent you are anticipating that the price momentum should last.

While some fundamental analysis of the securities can undoubtedly be valuable, you are hoping to distinguish circumstances where a specific security is probably going to move sensibly altogether in price over a generally short period. This depends on trends and patterns. When you have recognized that circumstance, you would then be able to buy or sell in like manner to profit from the price movements.

Options trading is achievable and utilizing most sorts of options. You can use different orders to take short positions or long positions on distinctive contracts. Options trading is much less serious than day trading and significantly less time-devouring. With day trading, you must be ready to spend the entire day checking the markets while trusting that the opportune time will enter and exit positions. The levels of attention required can be exceptionally depleting, and it requires an unmistakable range of abilities to utilize this style.

Options trading, then again, is an ideal center ground for those that need to see a sensibly fast return on their money yet don't have room schedule-wise to devote to buying and selling throughout the day, consistently.

It's an incredible style for those that are relative amateurs and those that have full-time occupations or have other time responsibilities amid the working day. It's feasible to emphasize potential swings and enter an important position. Check how your position is getting toward the finish of every day, or a couple of days, before choosing whether to exit that position.

Investigating and planning is essential for anybody hoping to utilize this style. You should be very ready and have a smart thought of precisely what sorts of examples and patterns you are searching for and what kind of transactions you will make in random circumstances. You want a level of flexibility in the manner in which you trade, though it can have an unmistakable arrangement of targets and a characterized plan for accomplishing those objectives. The market is unstable, and it will require you to make changes in like manner. A strong strategy gives you a platform to work from.

CHAPTER 1:

Getting Started with Options Trading

N ow with the necessary knowledge on options trading. There are a few details on how to start options trading journey.

Look for An Options Trading Broker.

The key to successful options trading is your broker. There exist legit and non-legit brokers in options trading. The following are some tips for selecting a good broker:

Do some research on the broker first. Be keen and alert before opening a brokerage options trading platform. Different brokers will approach you with different platforms. Do not rush or assume everything is functional; do some research on the best brokers. Make sure you spend your cash well by paying for a good options trading platform. It will help you a lot because your trading performance depends on your platform. Choose a broker with good ratings.

Charges lower commissions. Some brokers tend to exploit traders by charging high commissions to beginners. Weigh different commission offers of various brokers before settling on one. Some even charge no commission to traders. Prefer brokers with fewer commissions. Payment of high commissions periodically can mess you up with losses, and you may find it even hard to secure your trading capital. Do not accept to pay high commissions. You also need to do some savings other than wasting money while paying commissions.

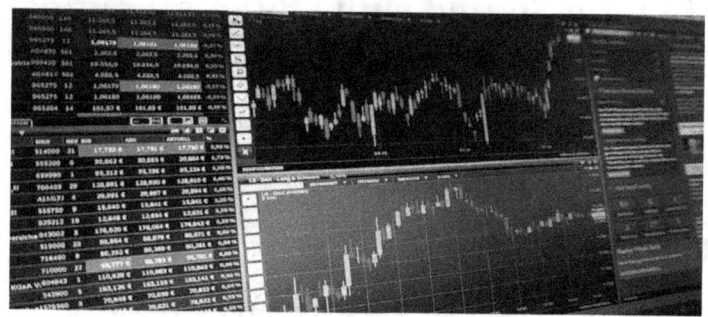

A simple user interface platform. There is a wide variety of software with different functionalities and features. Some software has a simple user interface, while others are too complex for you to use. Choose a platform with a simple and clear user interface that enables you to make your trades with less struggle. Some platforms can waste your precious time when you struggle too much searching on the Internet on how you operate them. Make your work easier by handling software that is according to your level. Trading tools for research. Consider factors like tools that are present on the platform. Do not purchase a platform with no tools. It will be hard for you. Platform tools ease your trading and make your performance excellent. The tools here may include charting tools, research tools, and even tools that alert you on any market changes that may arise.

Do Some Testing on The Brokerage Platform.

Do not be that kind of a careless trader who does things for the sake of doing with no precautions. You need to be cautious enough since this is an income-generating activity. You should test on a brokerage software before making up your mind of purchasing it. Check on the software's reliability and stability and be 100% sure that this is the platform you will use for your trading. Ensure the software is not that type of platform that crashes down unexpectedly. You might miss crucial trade while fixing your software.

Be Approved to Trade Options.

You need to be approved by the broker in charge before purchasing and offering options for sale. They usually have ways of passing you, like checking your experience and the money you have. It aids in avoiding risks for the customers. You cannot escape this step.

Get A Clear Understanding of The Technical Analysis.

Options trading is a specialized field. You need to have the special analysis techniques of trading options. The technical aspects include reading charts, know about the volume of stock, and also moving averages. Trading charts mostly analyze price behavior in the market. You will handle the aspects many times while trading. Perfect your technical knowledge and be cautious with them.

Take Advantage of Simulated Trading Accounts.

Using real accounts when starting options trading is a risky game. You can lose a lot of cash within a short time duration. Simulated accounts exist for a reason. You should test your trading skills in the mock accounts, learn a few tricks, and perfect your skills. The advantage of using a simulated account is that there is no loss of money since it mostly provides virtual money. When everything works out well, face real trading and shine.

Utilize Limit Orders.

It is risky to rely on market prices since price behavior change with time. A limit order enables you to purchase market securities at an agreed price. Using this type of order shuns you from incurring losses in options trading.

Revise Your Strategies with Time.

After entering into the options trading, with time, you need to revise your strategy. Utilize the working strategy more often and get rid of unsuccessful trading strategies. You should not have many plans that do not bring excellent performance. Few working strategies are better than having multiple ones that do not help you.

Register and Join in Options Trading Platforms.

Joining forums comprised of other options traders is another way of how to get started in options trading. Forums are platforms of different people with different experiences and opinions. You can learn mistakes made by others in trading. It is part of growing in options trading.

Study and Learn About Trading Metrics.

Having your returns maximized is also another way of getting started in options trading. Traders frequently use different trading metrics, such as delta, gamma, theta, and Vega. You should learn and practice them for massive returns.

CHAPTER 2:

Call and Put as Options Trading Fundamental

According to the rules governing options trading, whoever takes a purchase option on a house has not yet bought that house but has the option (the right) to buy the house within a specified period. In the financial markets, they pay an amount for an option to the person granting the right (the so-called option premium).

You cannot buy without a seller, so there are always two parties involved. The profit of one is losing another, and we call this a 'zero-sum game.'

However, both the buyer and the seller can earn money if the seller holds shares to cover the options. The profit on the shares then compensates for losing his option.

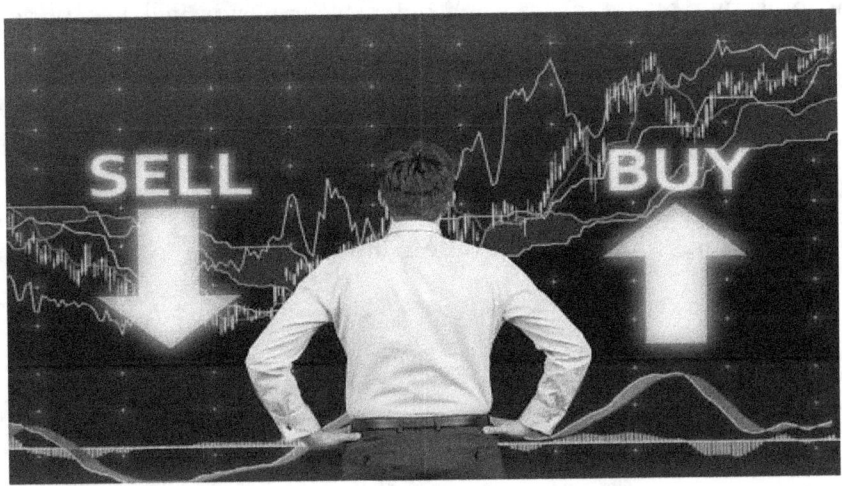

Call and Put

Call: A call has a right to an underlying buy at a convincing price within a specified period.

Sell: a sell is a right to an underlying asset to sell at a specific price within a certain period.

If you have a right, you can exercise it. If you have a duty, you are in a dependent position, and you have to wait for the counterparty to exercise its right. To acquire the privilege of the underlying, the buyer has to pay a premium to the seller (writer).

Remember, before entering a duty, you want a consideration, a payment, or a premium in money. Options are a standardized product so that everyone can trade them at the same time on equal terms. For example, the same specifications apply to your neighbor with the same option as you (although the costs per broker can differ).

Options can be applied both defensively and offensively, depending on the objective of an investor. A defensive investor will use options differently than an offensive trader.

It is precisely that aspect that makes options a product that deserves a place in every investment portfolio. Options are the best invention after the wheel. Like with a wheel, you can also roll options to a later expiry date.

Realize that you can either buy or sell options during the entire term and don't have to wait until the last trading day.

Buy and Sell Call Options

The big difference between buying or selling options is that you buy a premium when you buy options. You receive a premium when you write, so there is a risk that the counterparty, so the buyer, can exercise his option if the expiration option has value.

Long call (Buy a Call)

You can compare buying a call option with an option on a house: you may buy a house, for example, € 350,000 within a certain period. Suppose the house increases in value to € 400,000, you can exercise your purchase right, and you have a profit of € 50,000. In options trading, unlike a house, an option is not free, but the buyer must pay the price (the option premium) to the agent of the option.

Short call (Sell a Call)

The seller has an obligation (but not the right) to deliver a fixed amount of an underlying asset at the agreed price, the exercise price. Sellers calling an option can best be compared with an insurer who speculates on the do not pass a certain event: an underlying rise above a certain price. Before you invest in options, it is essential that you first learn what the options are, but more importantly, what the risks are. There are investment services that work with options and claim that you need not know about options, but that you have to follow their advice. We think it is better that you know what you are doing. If the entrepreneurs had bought those interest rate derivatives on their bank's help, they would have done so because they would not have suffered substantial losses.

CHAPTER 3:

Basic Option Trading Strategies

One way to ensure that you reduce risks is to find a good strategy that will help you pick out the right options and earn money. Many beginner investors who do poorly will often fail because they either didn't pick out an investment strategy initially or didn't understand and use that strategy properly. Picking out a strategy will help you choose which options to go with because it won't work with all of the options. The right strategy can also help determine how much risk you are willing to take when you first get started. It is essential to pick out a good investment strategy before you even talk to your broker or pick out any options to trade in. You are probably curious as to which options you should work with to see a good profit. Some of the best options trading strategies that you can pick include:

Covered call

This strategy is going to involve going in and purchasing the assets. Once you own the assets, you would write out a call option for them. This is used when the trader wants to earn some profits from their call premium, while also being able to protect against the possibility of the asset losing some value. With this one, if the volatility increases, the trader will lose, but if the volatility decreases, the trader will gain.

Naked call

This is a riskier strategy to work with, so if you are just getting started and want to keep your risks pretty low, this is probably not the best option for you to choose. With this option, the trader will sell a call option on the open market, but they don't own this asset. If the trade doesn't work out, it can cause you to lose a lot of money, but there are many gains as well if it is done properly.

Married Put

In this kind of option, the investor will purchase the asset they want to use while also doing a put option. It is a good choice because it will protect them against any short-term losses that may occur.

Bull call spread

Another strategy that an options investor can choose is the bull call spread. With this particular strategy, the trader will buy call options once a specific strike price is reached. When that strike price gets a bit higher (they will need to choose the right strike price that they want to use here), the trader will turn around and see the option and make a profit on the difference.

Bear put spread

You can also work with the strategy that is known as the bear put spread. This one is similar to what we say with the bull call spread, but a bit different because it goes the opposite way. This particular strategy involves purchasing a put option instead of at a specific strike price. Then when the strike price goes lower, they will sell the option. This is a strategy the trader would work with whenever they think the asset's price is going to go down. They can still make a profit from this as long as the price of the asset goes down. If it goes up, they stand to lose.

Protective collar

The trader is going to purchase an out of the money put option, and then at the same time, they will write an out of the money call option. This strategy is one that the trader will use when they see that the long position they have chosen is doing well. The protective collar allows the trader to lock in the profits they want without needing to sell the asset's shares.

Long straddle

The long straddle strategy is where the trader will pick out an option that they like and then buy a put and a call of this asset. Both orders are going to work on the same expiration date and strike price. This is the strategy you would want to use when the trader knows that their asset price will make a dramatic move sometime in the future, but they may be uncertain about which way the move will occur. This allows the trader to make money no matter which way the trade ends up going.

Long strangle

This one may look similar to the option that we had before, but there are a few differences that will make it unique. One difference is that while the put and the call options are going to be the same asset still and will use the same expiration date, they will come in with different strike prices. The price used with the call option will usually end up higher than the put strike's price, but both are going to be out of the money. This option is often less expensive than the long straddle, but it is a choice to go with when you think the asset's price will move up or down quite a bit soon.

Butterfly spread

This is a combination of a few strategies, and you may recognize a few points from the bear spread, and bull spread that we talked about earlier, which makes this one a bit more complicated. One method is going to purchase a call option at the strike price that is low as possible but, at the same time, selling two of your call options at a much higher strike price. Another option is to sell another call option with a higher strike price than the other two calls.

Iron Condor

For this strategy, the trader is allowed to hold the short and long positions simultaneously, but there has to be two separate strangles. It is an excellent way to get started with selling your options because you won't be able to experience a loss on both sides when you make this trade. It is a great way to get into the market when you only lose on one side while you win on the other.

Iron butterfly

When you want to have control over limiting your profits and losses within a range that you get to specify, this is a good strategy. It will help to cut your losses and make sure that you are limiting your risks. The trader will use what is known as an out of the money option. To work with this strategy, the trader will combine either a long or short straddle with a purchase or a strangle sale at the same time. This is different than the butterfly spread we just talked about because it will use both puts and calls.

CHAPTER 4

Methods of Buying Options

Buyers of call options view the marketplace cost of a specific stock and are looking to benefit from this predicted increase in market price.

The most well-known technique for buying call options is speculating on a boost in the market worth of the underlying stock. It is an essential strategy that is more popular than purchasing put options, as it is more easily comprehended.

Purchasing Options

When buying call options, you hypothesize that the rate of the underlying stock will increase substantially within the restricted time duration to produce a revenue. The percentage returns on your trade if you are proven proper are enormous. If you are incorrect, you can lose some or all of the premium initial you paid.

Buying the right to you is to purchase 100 shares of the underlying stock at the strike cost before the expiry date. You pay a premium for this right. Once you have bought your option, you have three options:

- Sell your Options before expiry.

- Exercise your options before expiration.

- Allow the option to expire worthlessly.

The action you take will rely on the movement in the market rate of the hidden share, your expectation of any future motion before expiry, your factors for purchasing the call, and your danger tolerance.

Time is a substantial aspect of figuring out how you manage your options trade. Everyday options that you hold, the value time of your option will decrease. And it will reduce at an increasing rate as you approach the expiration date. In truth, even if the market price of the underlying stock increases before expiry, you might still lose cash on your option due to the impact of time decay, counteracting any increase in intrinsic value.

Methods for purchasing call options

How can you have the money lost on your option when the market cost of the underlying stock has risen?

When you bought your option, it was at-the-money. As a result, the overall option premium of $3.50 consisted of time worth. Even though the stock cost increased by $2.00 and the intrinsic worth of your option increased by $2.00, this was offset by time decay of $3.50.

- Increase in intrinsic value$ 2.00.

- Decline in time value($ 3.50).

- Your net loss on the options *($ 1.50)

This estimation does not consist of deal costs. The above example shows that to earn a profit on buying a call OPTION, the marketplace worth of the underlying stock requirements to increase by enough to both:

- Balanced out the time decay.

- Create development in the intrinsic value of the option.

There are several factors why you may think about buying call options as your trading technique. These include the following:

Method 1: Gain Use

Purchasing call options give you the advantage in your profit. You only need to provide small capital to purchase call options compared to buying the stock entirely. It also allows you to increase the portion of your returns.

Method 2: Limit Your Danger

Getting call options, instead of acquiring the stock directly, also allows you to limit your losses if the stock cost falls. You might wish to speculate on a boost in the market worth of a specific stock; however, you might also not want to be exposed to prospective losses if the marketplace value falls considerably. If the stock you purchase, you are exposed to the full quantity of any fall in the stock cost. With call options, nevertheless, you can just ever lose the premium you paid, despite how far the stock rate might fall.

Method 3: Postpone A Stock Purchase

Once you buy a call option, you are purchasing the right to buy 100 shares of the primary stock at the strike price before the expiry date or anytime. Therefore, you are securing the rate you will pay for the shares if you decide to work out the option and buy it before the expiry date of the options.

You may want to invest long term in a specific stock as you feel it will increase in worth; nevertheless, for some factor, you wish to delay your purchase. Or perhaps you want to buy the stock however wishes to see it increase in worth to confirm your analysis of an anticipated price boost. Buying a call option permits you to postpone your purchase but still lock in the price at which you will acquire the stock. The marketplace has experienced some substantial falls in value recently, and you wish to take advantage of the price depressed. There is a stock single you have been watching before the fall, was trading over $30 per share and is now trading at merely $18 per share. You think that the cost will rebound; however, you do not have the funds offered.

You choose to buy a $19 call option that has five months to expiry. The premium is $1. This purchase lets you acquire the stock at $19 per share whenever in the following five months. You have five months to raise funds to purchase the shares and still purchase them at $19. Based upon what the stock rate does over this time, you can choose to offer your call options or exercise your call options and buy the stock at $19.

Method 4: Hypothesize for Profit

A significant factor for buying call options is hypothesizing to generate short-term revenue. You are just speculating on the cost of the underlying stock rising by enough total up to make earnings on your options. You are not acquiring the call options with any intent to exercise them.

Time decay will trigger the call options worth to fall as long as you are holding the option. For this factor, you need to be mindful of how you select the call options you wish to trade. You will require to stabilize the time you need for the stock to move in your instructions against the time value (expense) in the options premium.

You likewise require considering the strike price concerning the current market price of the stock underlying. You need options to be in-the-money to produce a boost in intrinsic worth. Call options will be more affordable when they are out-of-the-money, as more extensive price motion is needed to generate the option's inherent value. Conditions you should search for in selecting a call option for speculation consist of:

The strike price needs to be close to the current market value of the stock. When they are in-the-money options, this will ensure that the boost in the underlying stock cost will be shown in the price of your option.

The expiry time must be extended enough for your stock cost to increase adequately to balance out the time decay and create a profit on your call options.

CHAPTER 5:

Back Spread Strategy in Options Trading

An option is a very common derivative, as its price is less costly than other derivatives like the future. The stock of a blue-chip is a very flexible stock but very expensive. However, buying the blue-chip stock option might make a profit, just like buying the stock.

Investment and options trading seem like buying stocks. Because of the time value and expiry date of the contract, however, the buying of the naked contract is extremely risky.

If the stock price went down a lot after you purchase the naked option, after a certain time, even though the stock price is higher, the option price would still be below the demand price you used to buy this option.

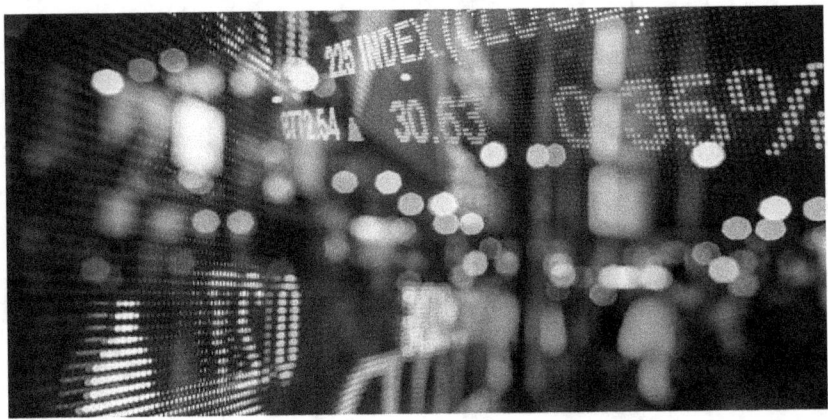

This is why we need an investment strategy or trade alternative. An option is a very effective method for investment and stock trading. By using the option, we could make use of the stock that moves up, down, and up. The option may also be used to execute an arbitrage strategy to gain a benefit, irrespective of the stock price up, down, or sideways.

The back spread is one of the most common option trading strategies. This strategy is similar to the so-called big and small gambling in China. When we play big, and the three dices after we shook and open show that the overall point is high, we will win 1-fold of money.

This means that if we stake 100, we can get another 100 back. Yet we're going to lose 100 if we lose. The back-spread strategy is pretty similar to this game. It means that if we spend 1000 USD, we can get another 1000 USD, or loss staked in it.

The estimated profit and loss are $1000. You're not going to risk anymore. The back spread is simply the reverse of the standard spread. The biggest benefit and loss are not necessarily the same. Often it varies a little and depends on the current stock price.

This strategy can be applied through the purchase of the money option and the selling of the money option. Since the price of the in-the-money option is greater than the out-of-the-money option, it is enough for the money earned by selling the out-of-the-money option.

But we do still have to position a deposit in our trading account, and the sum is usually the maximum loss that you will suffer if the stock price goes the other way. And if we expect the stock price to rise soon, we will buy the option of money and wealth.

If we expect the inventory price to fall soon, we will buy the cash and cash call option.

If we sell an option, we obtain a sum equal to the tender price, multiplied by the number of units purchased. The amount of money earned per option for a unit is USD 5.2, while the amount of money that we will pay per option for a unit is USD 2.7.

The net amount in your trading account is USD 2.5 per unit option after implementing this strategy. This means that your trading account must contain a USD 250 net.

Maximum profit/loss is as follows: maximum benefit = in - the-money bid price-Out - of-the-money option ask price Maximum loss = (top-level strike price = lower strike price)-(the in-the-money option bid price, out-of-the-money option ask price)

The bid price is USD 5.2, and the bid price out of money is USD 2.7. After both values have been replaced in the above calculations, we should learn that the maximum benefit is USD 2.5, and the maximum loss is USD 2.5.

If we, therefore, purchase one contract for each option in and out of money, the maximum benefit is USD 250, and maximum loss also amounts to USD 250. Breakeven point = Higher strike price = maximum benefit, or breakthrough points = lower strike price +

maximum loss may be used to determine the breakthrough point of that strategy.

In this case, the point of breakeven is 82.5. If the stock price rises above 82.5, we will benefit from this strategy. We will gain the full benefit only if we hold the position until the expiry date.

If we sell before the expiry date, we cannot make the full profit. But we can still earn money, just a little less than if we can hold the work until the expiry date. This is because the time value of the sell-out option is not fully acquired.

CHAPTER 6:

Intrinsic and Time Value in Options Trading

As an options trader, you need to learn about the variables that can affect the price of an option and the ins and outs of implementing the right strategy. A stock trader who is familiar and good with predicting future stock price movement might think that shifting to options trading is easy, but it's not. There are three changing parameters than an options trader must deal with – the underlying stock's price, the time factor, and volatility.

The premium is the price of an option, and the pricing is per share. The option seller receives the premium, which in turn gives the buyer any right that comes along with the option. The buyer is the one paying the premium to the seller, and they can exercise this right or allow the option to expire without any worth in the end. The buyer is obliged to pay the premium whether the option is exercised or not, which means the seller will keep the premium, in the end, no matter what.

Let's have a simple example. A buyer paid a seller for purchasing rights to stock ABC for 100 shares and a strike price at $60. The contract expires by June 19. If the option position becomes profitable, the option will be exercised by the buyer. If it does not seem to bear profit, the buyer can just let the contract expire. The seller then keeps the premium.

There are two sides to the premium of an option – its intrinsic and time value. You can compute for an option's intrinsic value by getting the difference between the strike price and stock price. For the call option, it is a stock price minus strike price. For the put option, it is a strike price minus the stock price.

To value an option, at least theoretically, you will need to consider multiple variables such as the underlying stock price, volatility, exercise price, time to expiration, and interest rate. These factors will provide you a good estimate on the fair value of an option that you can then incorporate into your strategy for maximum gains. The primary goal for option pricing is to compute the possibility that a particular option will be 'in the money' or exercised by the time it expires.

The value of puts and calls are affected by underlying stock price movements straightforwardly. When the price of a stock rises, there should be a corresponding rise in call value since you can purchase the underlying stock at a reduced price compared to the market's, while there is price decrease input.

There should be an increase in the value of put options when the price of the stock takes a dive, and a decrease in the value of call options since the holder of the put option has the option to sell the stock at above-market prices. This pre-set price at which you can sell, or buy is called the strike price of the option or its exercise price. If the option's strike price gives you the advantage of selling or buying the stock at a cost that gives you immediate profit, that option is considered 'in the money.'

Time

Time is money. This adage still holds true and even applies to options trading. Thus, understanding how the Greek theta works are very important and how it affects the pricing of options. If you still remember, the Greek letter theta represents the effect of time decay on the value of an option. All options, call or put, lose their value as the contract expiration nears, but the value loss rate of an option contract is a function of the amount of time remaining before it expires.

The outward part of the value of an option is the only factor affected by time decay. That means an option that's 'in the money' will have the same intrinsic value until the contract expires. If a stock trades at $3, a call for a 30-strike price will retain its intrinsic value of $3 from the start until expiration. Any value that exceeds $3 is considered extrinsic value and will be affected by the time decay.

Theta represents the loss of value over time, so a negative value typically represents it. And since time is irreversible, time only decreases and never stops or goes back. For example, if theta is set to -0.28, the corresponding option contract loses $0.28 in value daily.

However, theta does change over time. Let's assume that a stock's price remains unchanged, and a $2.75 'out of the money' option with a -0.15 theta will have a reduced value of $2.60 by the following day. The theta then may only be set to -0.12, which means the cost of the option will be down to $2.48 the succeeding day if stock prices remain unchanged. The option's value will gradually approach zero while it's still 'out of the money.'

You also need to remember that the effect of theta becomes more and more apparent as the expiration nears. You should anticipate a rapid acceleration of the time decay within the remaining few days before the contract expires.

Options that are 'at the money' possess the highest value, extrinsically. That's why these options have their thetas set to highest. Options that are 'in the money' or 'out of the money' have their thetas lower because compared to 'at the money options,' they have lower extrinsic values. And the less extrinsic value an option has, the less they will lose as time decays.

The only way for the theta position to be positive is to have short options. This is because short option positions work best when the market is stable. Wide swings both up or down hurt option positions, and only time will help as it passes by. Other strategies also benefit from time's passage, such as neutral strategies, e.g., long butterfly. The less time there is before the contract expires, the less probability for the underlying stock to rise or go down and reach unprofitable territories.

There will always be a trade-off between market movement and time for every option position. It's impossible to benefit from the two at the same time. If time is helping your option position, it will be negatively affected by the price movement. The same applies the other way around. Revisiting our Greeks, gamma (or price movement) is theta's flip side. A positive theta position (position benefitting from time's passage) will incur a negative gamma. Conversely, a position with a negative theta (position negatively affected by time's passage) will incur a positive gamma.

Volatility

Volatility affects most investment forms to some degree, and as an options trader, you should be familiar with this element and how it affects options pricing. By definition, volatility is the tendency of something to fluctuate or change significantly. In general investment, volatility refers to the rate of a financial instrument's price rises or falls.

A low volatility financial instrument has a relatively stable price. Conversely, a high volatility financial instrument is prone to dramatic price changes, either way. In general, financial market volatility can be broadly measured. So, when the market becomes difficult to predict, and prices keep on regularly and rapidly changing, the market is volatile

Volatility can affect option pricing significantly. Many beginning options traders tend to ignore the implications, which can lead to huge investment losses.

Before entering any trade, options trading included, it can be useful to have an idea about its volatility. For options, volatility is a key factor in how they are valued and priced. Two volatility types are relevant — historical volatility and implied volatility.

Historical Volatility

Historical or statistical volatility is used to measure the changes in the price of the underlying option, so it's based on actual and real data. Let's refer to it as HV for the rest. HV shows how fast the stock price has moved. The higher HV is, the more the stock price has moved during a certain period. So, when a stock has a high HV, the price is more likely to move, at least theoretically. It's more of a future movement indication and not a real guarantee.

On the other hand, a low HV might indicate the stock price hasn't moved much, but it might be going in one direction steadily.

You can use HV to predict somewhat how much a security's price will change based on how fast it changed in the past, but you can't use it to predict an actual trend.

HV is measured over a certain period, such as a week, month, or year and you can compute for it in various ways.

CHAPTER 7:

Inter-Market Analysis for Retail Asset Allocation

I t is a technique used by traders and investors to decide on the value of a stock or any other financial instrument by examining the factors that directly and indirectly affect a company's current and future business, financial, and economic prospects.

Inter market analysis endeavors to predict and learn the intrinsic value of securities such as stocks. An in-depth examination and analysis of certain financial, economic, quantitative, and qualitative factors will provide the solution.

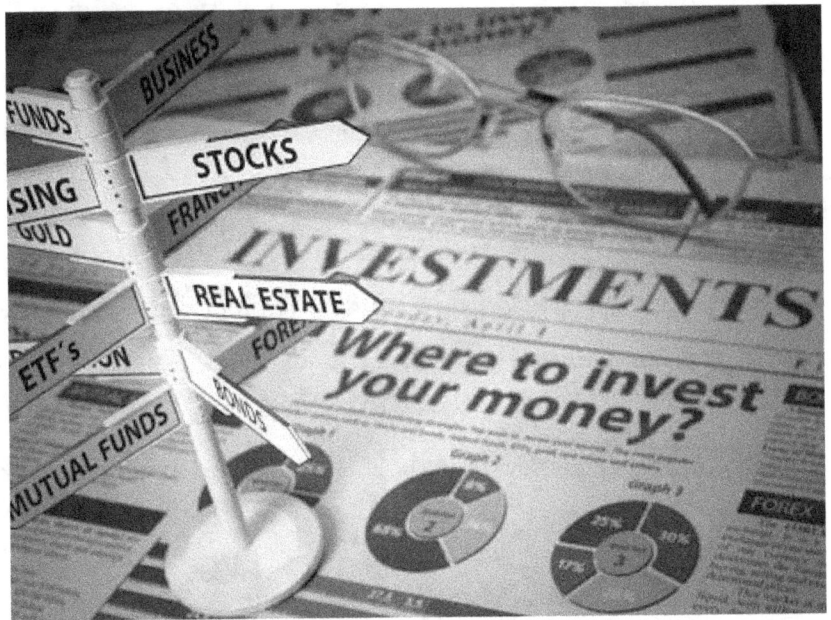

This fundamental analysis is mostly performed on a company so that trader can determine whether or not to deal with its stocks. It can also be performed on the general economy and particular industries such as the motor industry, energy sector, and so on.

Most of the fundamental analysis is conducted at a company level because traders and investors are mostly interested in information that will enable them to decide on the markets. They want information that will guide them in selecting the most suitable stocks to trade at the markets. As such, traders and investors searching for stocks to trade will resort to examining the competition, a company's business concept, its management, and financial data.

For a proper forecast regarding future stock prices, a trader must consider a company's analysis, industry analysis, and even the overall economic outlook. This way, a trader will be able to determine the latest stock price and predict future stock prices. When the outcome of fundamental analysis is not equal to the current market price, it means that it is overpriced or perhaps even undervalued.

Regarding stocks and options, the fundamentals include profit margins, price to earnings ratios, cash flow, and other indicators that give a picture of the company's overall health and prospects. The price of undervalued stocks is likely to increase at some point in the future, so spotting an undervalued stock could be useful for the swing trader.

It's also important to keep checking on company news of a more general nature. Suppose a product fails or ends up creating legal trouble for a company that can be an opportunity to short the stock or invest in put options. Alternatively, the release of a new product that exceeds expectations can be an opportunity to go long.

Price to Earnings Ratio

In the trading world, there are people who are known as market analysts. These are people who will often analyze how well companies are doing and then give the companies a review or a forecast, which allows other people to notice where the company is sitting. Market reviewers are typically known as cautious people and don't tend to believe that companies will pass their forecast.

This states that we need to look for stocks that have surprised the market analysts. This is because if companies pass their forecast, they will continue to succeed. Therefore, they become known as the best companies to gain a profit from, which is always a great thing for a trader to know.

Short Interest

This is the process that market analysts go through when they are evaluating how well a company is doing so, they can give them a forecast. These analysts are cautious and very careful to note where they think the company is going. Therefore, when the company goes farther than what they initially thought, they need to re-evaluate the company.

Earnings Momentum

While there are many important fundamental variables to look at when making an analysis, earnings momentum holds a special place. This variable is very important, especially when it comes to bull markets. Earnings momentum is the variable that looks at the year to year growth of earnings. Therefore, this is what will often set the price for stocks.

Earnings Growth

Another variable you want to pay attention to is how much more money the company is making as the years go on. When you look at this variable, you will be looking at the earnings growth variable. This is another company that you would think of investing in because you know that they have seen considerable growth for a certain number of years. Therefore, you analyze that the company will only continue to grow.

If you want to be a successful stock trader, a swing trader, or an analyst, you must learn about fundamental analysis. It is the most crucial aspect of any investment or trading strategy. Many would claim that a trader is not accomplished if they do not perform fundamental analysis.

The fact is that fundamental analysis is such a broad subject that what it entails sometimes differs depending on scope and strategy. It involves many things such as regulatory filings, financial statements, valuation techniques, and so on.

Total Revenue

A company's total revenue is important and can be easily understood by investors with limited financial knowledge. This revenue number is a measure of a company's total sales of their products or services. It is often a good indicator that a company is doing well if its revenue is growing steadily year over year. If the revenue numbers are flat or dropping year over year, it shows that a company is probably having trouble growing its business and that profits will likely be flat or dropping. Falling profits usually translate to a falling stock price.

As a swing trader, you can check to see if the stock you are considering for a position has growing or declining revenues and determine if that is aligned with your trade. For example, are you going long on a stock with growing total revenue numbers?

Earnings per Share

Earnings are calculated by taking the total revenue and subtracting the direct costs of production. Positive earnings are important in the long term for any business to continue operating. However, the name "earnings" should not be confused with profit or profitability. Profits are calculated by subtracting the additional costs of doing business, such as interest paid on debt. At some point in a company's history, it will need to start turning a profit, or investors will lose patience, funds will run out, and bankruptcy will follow.

Debt to Equity

Most companies need funds to start up and operate their business. They need money to pay employees, to purchase inventory, to buy equipment and computers, etc. That money can come from 2 sources: debt and equity.

Debt is essentially borrowed money that the company usually pays interest for its use. The debt will also need to be repaid at some point in time. Equity is money invested in the company, and, in return, the investor is given shares. Those shares represent some percentage of ownership in the company. At some point, the investor hopes to sell their shares for a profit and collect dividends, which are payments that come from the company's profits.

Debt and equity represent different levels of risks for a company and its shareholders. Debt comes with obligations to pay interest and repay the outstanding loan at some point. Therefore, it is a higher risk to the company than equity, which has no such obligations. Equity has more risk for the shareholders because if the company goes bankrupt, the debt holders usually get first pick at whatever is left of value. The equity investors get what is leftover, and that is usually nothing.

CHAPTER 8:

Weekly Options Trading

W eekly options are listings that provide an opportunity for short-term trading as well as plenty of hedging possibilities. As the name states, they have an expiration time of exactly one week; in general, they are listed on Thursday and expire the following Friday. They have primarily been the domain of investors who work with cash indices. This exclusivity level changed in 2011 when the Chicago Board of Options expanded the number of ways they could be traded, especially to make them more easily acceptable to traders like you. Since then, the number of stocks that can be traded weekly has grown from 28 to nearly 1,000.

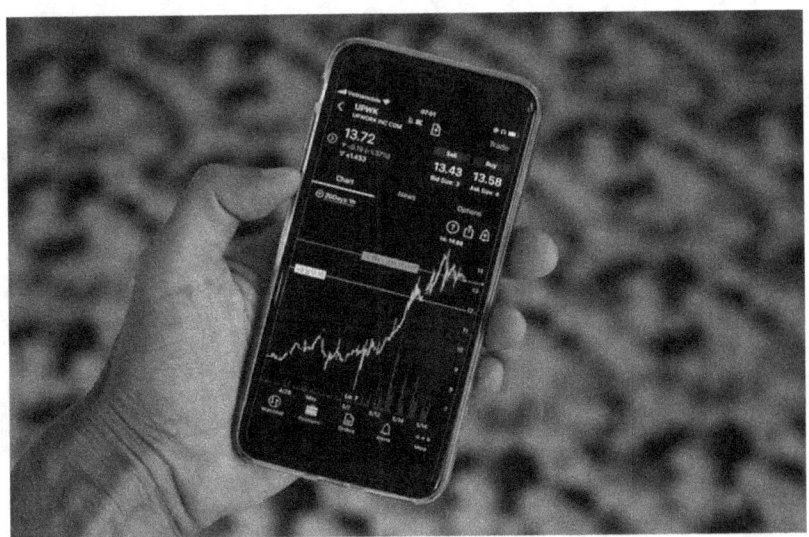

The biggest benefit of buying into weekly options is that you are free to purchase what you need for the exact trade you are looking to make without having to worry about coming up with extra capital or dealing with more options than you currently need. This means if you are looking to start a swing trade, or even an intraday trade, weekly options will have you covered. For those looking to sell, weekly options provide the ability to do so more frequently, rather than wait a month between sales.

Weekly options trades are also useful in that they lead to reduced costs for trades that have longer spreads, such as diagonal spreads or calendar spreads, as they can sell weekly options against them. They are also useful to higher volume trades as they are useful when it comes to hedging larger positions and portfolios against potential risky events. Also, when the market is range-bound the weekly options, the market can still be utilized through means such as the iron butterfly or iron condor.

The biggest disadvantage when it comes to weekly options is that you will not ever have very much time for a trade to turn around if you make the wrong choice in the first place. If you are selling options, then you will also need to know that their gamma will also be much more sensitive than it would be with more traditional options. This means that if you are planning to short options, then a relatively small move overall can still lead to an out of the money option entering into the money very quickly.

Weekly options are also known to require a good deal more micromanaging of risk. Without taking the time to size your trades and guarantee your profits properly, you will find that your available trade balance disappears quickly. The implied volatility of all trades is going to much higher than it would have been otherwise due to the time frame you are dealing with. Near term, options are always going to be more open to large price swings as well.

Buying weekly: Because you are always going to have much less time when it comes to turning a profit with a weekly option, your timing for when to move on a specific decision needs to be much more precise than it would otherwise have to be. If you choose poorly at either strike selection, time frame or price direction, then you can easily find yourself paying for a generally worthless option. You will also need to take your level of acceptable risk into account as the option is going to be cheaper, but you will need to purchase more in a week than you otherwise would.

Selling weekly: Selling reliably for the long-term can generate steady profits if done properly. It is important always to know what your options are worth to prevent you from selling yourself short. Selling trades weekly will make it easier to collect the full premium if they correctly while still leaving you exposed to unmitigated losses if you choose poorly, which requires an extra margin.

The ideal types of the underlying stock to use for these types of trades will be lower priced as they each ultimately consume a smaller amount of your total buying power. This also means it is easier to move forward on trades with lots of implied volatility, as it is more likely to revert to the mean in the allotted time. As a rule, selling a put in the short-term is always better than selling a call as it tends to generate an overall higher return in the shorter period.

Spreads: Spreads are a great way of making a profit in the weekly market. The overall level of implied volatility is going to be much higher in the weekly market than in the monthly variation. The spread can help you when you find yourself dealing with an unexpected directional change quickly enough that you can do something about it. Selling an option against a long option will naturally decrease the role volatility plays in the transaction. The best point to use the debit spread will be near where the price currently is, providing you with a 1 to 1 risk and reward ratio.

CHAPTER 9:

Trade Performance Metrics Portfolio Measures

D ay traders generally execute trades in the course of a single trading day while investors buy and hold stocks for days, weeks, months, and sometimes even a couple of years. It is recommended to take the option of diversifying trading accounts, and other than day trading options strategies seriously, add a mid or long-term approach to get fewer fluctuations in the overall portfolio. That's why you will learn here the basics of portfolio diversification. If you are a complete beginner, using only day trading strategies will expose you to huge loss over a long time, due to large intrinsic leverage of options and day trading strategy in general.

A trader with the necessary skills and access to all the important resources is bound to succeed and encounter a steep learning curve. Professional day traders work full time, whether working for themselves or large institutions. They often set a schedule which they always adhere to. It is never wise to be a part-time day trader, a hobby trader, or a gambler. To succeed, you have to trade on a full-time basis and be as disciplined as possible. Diversification is considered an effective risk management technique. Both traders and investors widely use it. The gist behind this approach is that investing funds in just single security is extremely risky as the entire trade could potentially go up in smoke or incur significant losses.

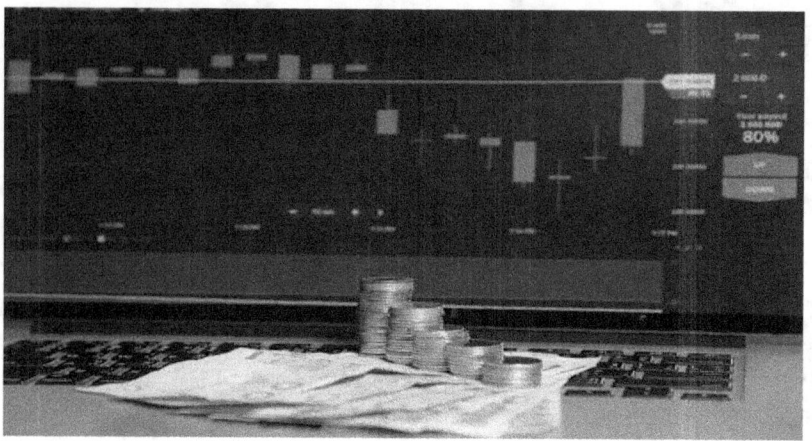

An ideal portfolio of securities is expected to fetch a much higher return compared to a no-diversified portfolio. Generally, diversification is advisable not only because it yields better returns but also because it offers protection against losses.

Diversification Basics

Traders and investors put their funds in securities at the securities markets. One of the dangers of investing in the markets is that traders are likely to hold onto only one or two stocks at a time. This is risky because if a trade was to fail, then the trader could experience a catastrophe. With diversification, the risk is spread out so that regardless of what happens to some stocks, the trader still stands to be profitable.

At the core of diversification is the challenge posed by unsystematic risks. When some stocks or investments perform better than others, these risks are neutralized. Therefore, for a perfectly balanced portfolio, a trader should ensure that it only deals with non-correlated assets. This means that the assets respond in opposite ways or differently to market forces.

The ideal portfolio should contain between 25 and 30 different securities. This is to ensure that the risk levels are drastically reduced, and the only expected outcomes are profitability.

Diversification is a popular strategy that is used by both traders and investors. It uses a wide variety of securities to improve yield and mitigate inherent and potential risks.

It is advisable to invest or trade in a variety of assets and not all from one class. For instance, a properly diversified portfolio should include assets such as currencies, options, stocks, bonds, and so on. This approach will increase the chances of profitability and minimize risks and exposure. Diversification is even better if assets are acquired across geographical regions as well.

Best Diversification Approach

Diversification focuses on asset allocation. It consists of a plan that endeavors to allocate funds or assets appropriately across a variety of investments. When an investor diversifies his or her portfolio, there is some level of risk that has to be accepted. However, it is also advisable to devise an exit strategy so that the investor can let go of the asset and recoup their funds. This becomes necessary when a specific asset class is not yielding any worthwhile returns compared to others.

If an investor can create an aptly diversified portfolio, their investment will be adequately covered. An adequately diversified portfolio also allows room for growth. Appropriate asset allocation is highly recommended. It allows investors a chance to leverage risk and manage any possible portfolio volatility because different assets have varying reactions to adverse market conditions.

The Process of Asset Class Allocation

There are different ways of allocating investments to assets. According to studies, most investors, including professional investors, portfolio managers, and seasoned traders rarely beat the indexes within their preferred asset class. There is a visible correlation between an underlying asset class's performance and the returns that an investor receives. In general, professional investors tend to perform more or less the same as an index within the same class asset.

Investment returns from a diversified portfolio can generally be expected to imitate the related asset class closely. Therefore, asset class choice is considered an extremely crucial aspect of an investment. It is a single, more crucial aspect for the success of a particular asset class. Other factors, such as individual asset selection and market timing, only contribute about 6% of the variance in investment outcomes.

Wide Diversification between Various Asset Classes

Diversification to numerous investors simply implies spreading their funds through a wide variety of stocks in different sectors. These include health care, financial, energy, and medium caps, small and large-cap companies. This is the opinion of your average investor. However, a closer look at this approach reveals that investors are simply putting their money in different stocks class sectors. These asset classes can very easily fall and rise when the markets do.

A reliably diversified portfolio is where the investor or even the manager is watchful and alert because of the hidden correlation between different asset classes. This correlation can easily change with time, and there are several reasons for this. One reason is international markets. Many investors often choose to diversify their portfolios with international stocks.

Realignment of Asset Classes

One of the best approaches to solving the correlation challenge is to focus on class realignment. Asset allocation should not be considered as a static process. Asset class imbalance is a phenomenon that occurs when the securities markets develop, and different asset classes exhibit varied performance.

After a while, investors should assess their investments then diversify out of underperforming assets and instead shift this investment to other asset classes that are performing well and are profitable in the long term. It is advisable to be aware so that no one single asset class is over-weighted as other standard risks are still inherent. Also, a prolonged bullish market can result in overweighting one of the different asset classes which could be ready for a correction.

CHAPTER 10:

Vertical Spread strategy

When it comes to spread trading, there are two categories all types of trades fit into. These are vertical spreads and horizontal spreads. The names sound fancy but understanding how they work really isn't anywhere near as complicated.

Having said that, these types of trades do crank the complexity level up a bit. If the collar took things up a notch from covered calls then spread trades do the same with the collar.

As beneficial as collars and covered calls are there is one major disadvantage that those strategies pose to the trader.

They require a long stock purchase. In the covered call this is an investment while in the case of a collar it can be speculative or an investment. Whatever the designation there's no escaping the fact that long stock investment requires a lot of money.

This is what the spread strategies address. Options give us the flexibility to play around with the way price moves and as you'll see, spread trades encompass taking advantage of a wide variety of market behavior.

Bull Call Spreads

The first type of vertical spread we'll be looking at is the bull call spread. This is a bullish trading strategy and works best in the middle portions of trending markets. I'll address why this is so. For now, keep in mind that while this is a bullish strategy it works best when bullishness is beginning to slow down, and you observe the ranges getting larger.

You can utilize this in the earlier, more forceful, part of trends but this isn't the most efficient use of it. In those portions, you're better off simply buying a call and letting its premium rise. The covered call works well in those environments too.

Either way, the bull call spread has two legs to it. You will be buying one call and selling another. Thus, the long call leg of the trade covers the short call. Let's take a look at the legs in more details

Trade Legs

The first leg you should establish is the long call leg. This needs to be an at the money or out of the money call that you're sure will move into the money soon. The objective is to use this leg to make the majority of the profit in this trade.

Establishing a long stock position meant that you needed to protect it somehow which is why we had to incorporate a third leg in the case of the collar. With the covered call, given the investment nature of the trade, downside protection is moot since you'll be holding onto it for the long term anyway and the objective is to hold onto your investment no matter how much it dips (assuming the dip isn't catastrophic.)

The second leg of the bull call spread is the short call. This is written out of the money at a point where you think the price will advance to, even if it does so sluggishly. Much like with every other strategy we've looked at, you want both of these options to expire at least 30 days or more from the trade date. This helps you capture and avoid the risk of time decay.

Like the collar, the bull call spread can be adjusted, and its greatest power lies in a good adjustment. This allows you to remain in the market at a low cost. Adjustments depend on what the market scenario looks like. As I mentioned earlier, you should deploy this in times when bullishness is starting to be challenged by bearishness and thus, you will enter with the knowledge that the trend is still strong but there are some headwinds ahead.

You should place your short call at a level beyond the most relevant resistance ahead. Once price breaches this level, you should move it a few points higher to where the next resistance level could potentially be and so on. Alternatively, you could let the market take you out of the position and close your long and cover your short position if you feel that the counter trend presence is becoming far too much.

Bull Put Spread

The bull put spread strategy seeks to take advantage of the exact same set of market conditions that the bull call spread seeks. One strategy uses calls and the other uses puts, there are many subtleties that you ought to be aware of.

The strategies do not contradict one another, in case you're wondering. Think of it as having two choices to pursue depending on what market conditions look like. If you're wondering how to determine the conditions which are ideal for each strategy, take a look at the bull put spread and understand how it works.

Trade Legs

Like the bull call, the bull put is a two-legged trade. The first leg involves establishing a long-put position that is out of the money and is below a strong support level. This long put is what caps your downside risk in case things go wrong. In addition to this, the long put also covers the next leg.

This is a short put which is written near or at the money. This leg is the primary profit driving instrument for the trade. I'd like to point out here that the structure and positioning of the puts are very different from that of the calls. With the bull call spread, you were capping your maximum gain on the trade by writing an OTM call.

Here's you're not capping any gains and are in fact capping your loss via a trade leg. In the bull call spread, your maximum loss was automatically capped as a part of the trade structure. You could argue that this is what is happening here as well but it's pretty clear that the way in which the strategies do this is very different.

The major point of difference is in the results trade entry gives you. The bull call is net debit trade, but the bull put is a net credit trade. Net debit trades have you realize your maximum loss upon trade entry. Net credit trades realize your maximum gain upon entry. This means, you earn your maximum profit on entry and if all goes well, your options will maintain themselves.

Like the bull call spread, you can adjust the trade depending on market conditions. Given that your upside is not capped, adjustments will need to be made primarily if the market turns downwards and if you see your puts move into the money. In this case, you will need to readjust the spread lower and exit your primary position. Thus, the adjustment scenarios in the bull put strategy aren't as varied as they are in the others we've seen so far.

You can establish a higher spread using the same principles you used if the trade works in your favor.

CHAPTER 11:

Getting a Trading Hedge in Options Trading

U sing options to hedge your portfolio is a very cost-effective way to get the protection in place. To hedge your investment portfolio, you will need to buy a put option. A put option gives you the right to sell a fixed amount of stock, at an agreed price, at a future date. The agreed price in an option is called the strike price. The price that you pay to purchase a put option is called the premium. If the market falls, then you will be able to sell the options back to the market and use the profit to offset any loss that you suffered on your investment portfolio.

In most cases, assuming the equity part of your portfolio is made up of good quality American stocks, the best option is to purchase a put option against an index such as the S&P 500. This will cover movements in all of your stocks to a greater or lesser extent, but overall should be approximately in line with the movement of the equity part of your portfolio. As index options are always cash settlement, so you never have to worry about dealing with the stock part of the option. Index options also enjoy favorable tax treatment, as they qualify for 60% long term, and 40% short term, capital gain treatment. This applies to all index linked options such as the Dow Jones and the NASDAQ.

An important step is to use an index to hedge your portfolio to figure out which index suits your portfolio's composition best. If your portfolio is large, high capitalization companies, such as Cisco, Microsoft, Exxon, and General Electric, then more than likely, S&P index options will be your best bet. If you are more heavily invested in smaller capitalization stocks, or even mid-sized companies, there is less chance that the S&P index will accurately reflect movements in your portfolio. This means that your hedge will not be as effective, and even if you did it at the correct time, it may not save you as much as it should. For a portfolio of smaller stocks, consider using the Russell 2000 or S&P Midcap 400 indices. Track your portfolio's performance against different indices, long before you want to hedge, to get a sense of which index will best suit your needs.

Example of an Option Hedge

To calculate the size of the hedge that you need. Assuming your portfolio is worth $1 million, with 60% invest in equities, you will need to hedge $600,000. You need to consider how much you want to spend. In this example, you only want to spend 3% of your total investment, to protect it from a fall in value, for the following three months. This is a total of $18,000.

Calculate also how many options you can afford to buy. An index put option gives you the right to sell 100 issues of S&P "stock." Assuming the S&P is at 1,900, and a 3-month S&P option has a strike price of 1,900, with an asking price of $45. Then one option will cost $45 * 100 S&P index stocks so $4,500. Given your budget of around $18,000, you need to buy four options. The cost of the put option will be high because it protects you against any loss in the value of your portfolio.

This table will show how your option purchase hedges your portfolio against changes in S&P's value. You will notice the portfolio value includes the $18,000 cost of the options, so it is $582,000 instead of $600,000.

S&P % Change	S&P Value	Value of Options	Portfolio Value	With Options	Hedged % change
5%	1995	0	$599,460	$599,460	-0.02%
0%	1900	0	$582,000	$582,000	-3.00%
-5%	1805	$38,000	$552,900	$590,900	-1.50%
-10%	1710	$76,000	$523,800	$599,800	-0.01%

You can see that the hedge works very effectively, as the value of your portfolio barely changes. For a 5% decline in the S&P index, the value of the option rises. The calculation is (1900-1805*100), so a profit of

$9,500 for each option you purchased. You would have to pay a commission on this hedge, so it would not work quite well. Also, note that you still do not reach the original $600,000 value of the portfolio, even if it rises by 5%.

This is the problem with hedging, as it reduces your profits in an upswing, but you can sell the options back to the market, if the market starts to rise, before it reaches a 5% increase, allowing you to benefit from the upswing. If the market did drop by the 5% you expected, then your hedged loss is $600,000 – $590,900 = $9,100 versus an un-hedged loss of $600,000 - $552,900 = $47,100. If it had dropped further, you would almost make a profit instead of a loss.

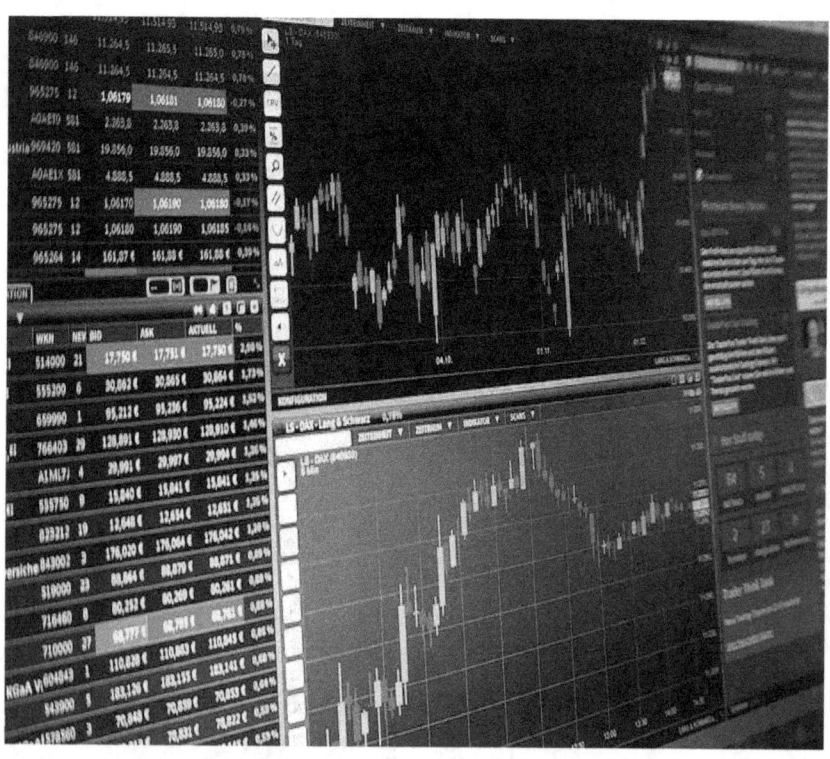

CHAPTER 12:

Evaluation of Variables in Options prices

It is not possible to price an option unless an individual understands what constitutes its value. This is because a single option trade can morph into a complex process of adjustments, multiple orders, and several strategies. In the broader sense, options prices are made up of two key components, i.e., time value and intrinsic value.

Time value is any amount that is more than the intrinsic value of the option. On the other hand, the intrinsic value is the difference between the underlying price of an option and its strike price. Therefore, options that have intrinsic value are those that are in-the-money. This can be summarized as follows:

- The intrinsic value of a call option = underlying price minus strike price

- The intrinsic value of a put option = strike price minus the underlying value.

Traders can use options for several different strategies, from high risk to conservative, to achieve objectives that go beyond standard directional strategies. It is essential to learn and understand the key influencers on options prices in different scenarios. Changes in any or all of these influences will affect the value of an option.

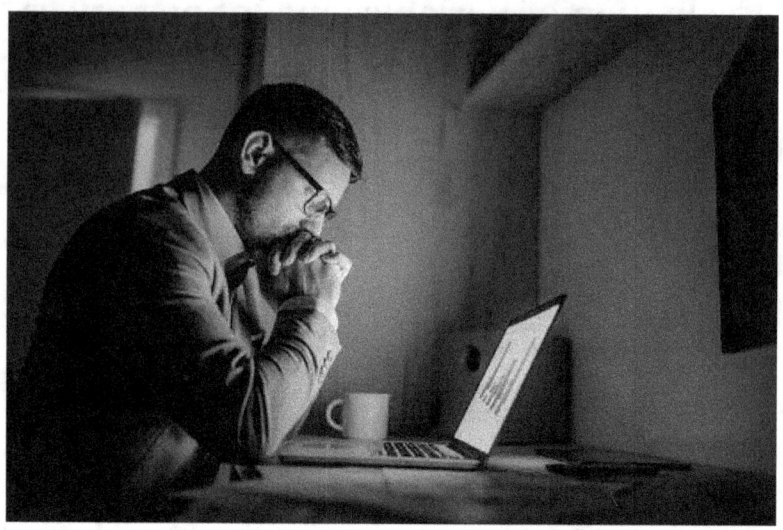

Valuation Models

The valuation model used will affect the price of the options. There is a difference between theories of options pricing and options valuation. For example, the Black-Scholes model and similar pricing models attempt to determine the value of an option that makes it consistent with the price of the underlying security or asset. These theories assume a business environment where a riskless, dynamic arbitrage strategy with the option and stock or asset is possible, thereby determining the option value as an aspect of the arbitrage portfolio.

According to this ideal market environment, if the model value differs from the option's value, the option value can be traded against the number of shares of stock to identify a position that is relatively free of risk. Constant rebalancing will help keep the position free of risk until the expiration date of the option. However, applying these models in real-world trading can be quite challenging, especially if an individual is not adequately experienced in options trading.

In trying to apply these theoretical valuation models, a trader will conclude that none of them works as expected. The strategy outlined above, which is supposed to be costless and riskless in theory, is not in practice. This is because positions cannot be continuously balanced when markets are closed. Also, failing to rebalance continuously will lead to transaction costs. These theories also depend on stock volatility, which cannot be predicted exactly.

It is important to understand that these theoretical valuation models offer some valuable assumptions about pricing that are important for options traders to understand; therefore, they should not be taken for granted.

It is important to understand how options are priced to make smarter and more profitable plays and decisions. To understand how they are priced; options traders need to note the following pricing considerations and assumptions based on common valuation theories:

- The underlying price of an option is normally distributed

- There are no restrictions to short selling

- All securities are desirable, and there are no taxes and transaction costs

- No arbitrage opportunities are risk-free

- During the life of the derivative asset, there are no dividends

- For all maturities, the risk-free rate of interest is the same and constant

- Prices can trade in a continuous manner

Underlying Asset Price

This is the first influencer on the price of an option. For each underlying asset, there are several options at varying price increments, also referred to as strike price, which is the predetermined price that will apply if the option is exercised. For example, if a trader owns company XYZ stock at $100 per share, he or she could purchase the 100-put since that is where he or she could sell his or her shares in case the company's stock drops in value, and he or she decides to exercise the option.

An options trader does not have to hold or own shares in a company to trade options; however, the share's strike price will have a significant impact on the option price. For example, for calls, if company XYZ's current stock price is $100 per share, any option that has a strike price higher than $100 is considered to be in-the-money, which is the opposite for put options.

Out-of-the-money options, on the other hand, have no value at expiration. Therefore, if they have no value at the expiration date, an individual might wonder why it has a value before expiration. It is because the price of stock changes, and there is a good chance that the out-of-the-money options could become in-the-money if there is still some time remaining before expiration.

Volatility

Another factor that goes into options pricing is volatility, which refers to the magnitude of a security's price fluctuations. Extreme volatility leads to extreme price swings and subsequently, more risk for stock owners. Different securities have different levels of volatility; however, this fluctuation in price is not constant. This means that a stock that currently has low volatility might become more volatile in the future.

It is much easier to predict volatility than stock price; therefore, options traders need to place themselves on the profitable side of volatility. However, its effect on an option price is one of the most difficult concepts for novice traders. A trader needs to look at past stock price movements over a certain period to determine its effect, referred to as statistical volatility or historical volatility.

CHAPTER 13:

Analyzing Market Trend in Options Trading

A bullish market is characterized by a succession of lower and higher points, and higher and higher points. In a clear uptrend, the corrective phases (drop legs) are less important in amplitude than the impulsive phases (legs of rising). It provides a valuable indication of the possibility of a trend reversal.

When a corrective leg has a greater amplitude than the impulsive leg (bullish in a bull market), the uptrend is likely to be challenged.

The trader will have to reconsider the current trend and avoid positioning himself for the purchase.

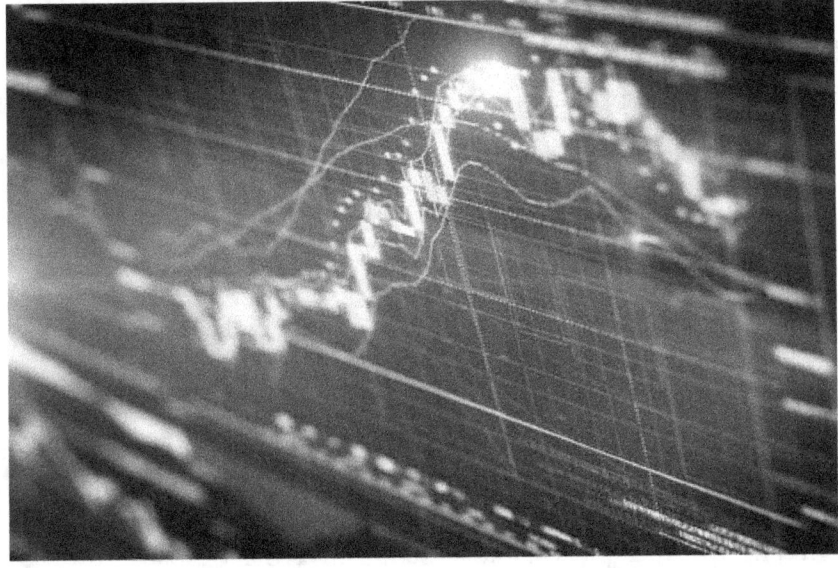

A downtrend market is characterized by lower and higher points, but also by lower and lower points. In this type of market, rebounds often have less amplitude than bearish legs, the main characteristic of a bear market.

In a trending market, the movements that go in the direction of the dominant trend are still the most powerful.

As for the uptrend, the turnaround can be anticipated. This requires the recovery to be larger than the last bearish wave.

The Market without Trend

There is no clear trend in a trendless market, and low points and high points are often confused. Buyers and sellers are testing themselves, and no clear consensus is at work.

According to Wilder, markets evolve in trend one-third of the time and do not draw any clear trend during the remaining two-thirds. This property is important because investors are often victims of momentum bias. They tend to prolong the recent course evolution mechanically. If the course progresses during the last sessions, they are convinced of the continuation of its rise, and many traders are trapped by positioning themselves around resistance or slightly above. Investors say that the decline in stock prices will continue and are trapped by opening a position around major support.

The good trader can wait patiently for the right moment before opening a position. Professional traders seek to position themselves at the beginning of an impulsive movement and avoid exposure by taking unnecessary risks when the market is not predictable. Good traders are people who can adapt to changing market conditions. Markets fluctuate differently depending on whether we are in an uptrend, bearish trend, or a trending market. In a bullish (bearish) market, the trader will be able to afford to buy (sell) up (down) and sell (buy) even higher (low), even if that is not ideal.

Trend Lines

This is used by traders to identify bullish points in an uptrend and highs in a downtrend. In a bull market, the trend line goes through at least two low points. Conversely, in a downtrend market, the trend line will join at least two high points. It is possible to adjust trends over time based on new information: sharper, more marked trends may indeed appear as the trend initially traced becomes obsolete.

Conditions of Effectiveness of a Trend Line

Their effectiveness justifies the success of trend lines in identifying good levels of support and resistance. In other words, they sometimes make it possible to give surprisingly precise these minor levels of reversal when a trend has already started. The possibility of identifying the state of the trend and anticipating reversals or simply corrective movements.

Finding a Trend Reversal Using a Trend Line

The rupture of a trend line is an important reversal signal. This signal is all the stronger as the trend line is significant (it has been used on many occasions to support the current trend). The break of a bullish or bearish straight line materializes the end of a market dynamic: the operators who should have strengthened their positions near the trend line proved to be weaker than the opposing side (the bearers), thus allowing the rupture of the right and all the dynamics of the market. The change in trend thus seems clear.

A broken bullish straight line immediately becomes a line of resistance against which the market will crash; this is often shown by a pullback (return to the right of a trend that has just been broken). The market is thus testing the strength of the support that has become resistant (or vice versa). Beware; the break of a trend line cannot alone constitute a signal of a reversal of the market, as shown by the example of the title PPR. It only alerts the trader about the possibility of consolidation.

Canals or Channels

A channel (Canal) is a figure directly related to the analysis of trend lines. The tracking is simple: once a bullish trend has been determined, it is a question of finding a parallel to the tendency to cover all the evolution of prices. Over the period when the trend is observed (straight line connecting the extreme points), we obtain a channel in which the courses evolve harmoniously.

The channel will tuck into a trend by allowing impulse turning points to be determined through trend lines and corrective turning points through the upper channel of the uptrend channel - or the bottom line for a downtrend channel.

The courses vary between these two lines: the first constitutes the support line of the canal, where the courts come to rest; the second represents the resistance line of the channel (or top of the channel) against which the market stumbles.

As for trends, it is possible to distinguish short, medium, and long-term channels. The importance of a channel depends on the duration of evolution, and the number of times each line of the channel has been affected. To be considered a canal, you need at least two impacts on each side.

Intermediate Lines

prices do not move stubbornly between the lower bound and the upper bound. They sometimes have trouble passing intermediate areas within the canal. You can draw parallel straight lines to the channel, which constitute many lines of support or minor resistance for the courses. However, the number of real intermediate rights is limited; one generally finds only one, even two. They are often halfway through the channel and are real tests to know if the courses will reach the top or bottom. In the case of a bullish channel, the break in the intermediate resistance line often indicates that the market will reach the top of the channel.

How to Detect the End of a Trend?

Can trend reversals be identified using chart analysis? It is necessary to have a clear trend, for example, a trend line whose impulsive movements have a greater amplitude than corrective movements. The breaking of a major trend line or major support is often a precursor signal of reversal. The various researches show that a figure of large turnaround (thus which took some time to be formed) will often be at the origin of an important corrective movement.

Trends are a common phenomenon in the markets, but operators often misunderstand their training. Dow has developed a theory to provide relevant explanations for this phenomenon and can be applied to current markets, regardless of the period used.

CHAPTER 14:

The Basics of Trading Stock Options

S tocks are some of the ownership of the business you finance with the companies. You have a right to have the earnings of the company in which you hold the shares. The higher the shares, the more ownership you have in the business.

A person who has its stocks in some organization does not own the whole firm. But he has some of the shares of the company. He has no right to the corporation's offices or the properties or other assets the company owns. The laws for the company and the shareholders are separate. For instance, if the company goes bankrupt, the shareholders are not supposed to sell their shares.

However, the worth of the shares will markedly go down. The same goes for the corporation; if the shareholders are bankrupt, they are not allowed to sell the company's assets to pay off his creditors.

Owning some of the stocks does not mean that you own a company. Having the shares means you have the right to claim for the profit, the company is gaining. You will get more advantage if you own more extensive stocks. You can either buy the shares from the company itself, it is the primary market, or buy it from other shareholders, known as the secondary market.

Types of Stocks

When the company is established, there is usually a small number of investors and founders. For instance, a company started, and it has one investor and two founders, so three of them have probably equal values of the shares. But as the company expands, it needs more capital for its growth. So, the company sells its shares to other shareholders, resulting in a lower percentage of shares for the prior shareholders.

As the company grows further, it needs more investment, and the previous investors choose to sell their shares to make their profits legal. As the company needs a high investment that a private investor cannot afford, the firm decides to transform the company from private into a public corporation. There are mainly two types of stocks, common stocks and preferred stocks.

Common Stock

A major part of the stocks is issued as common stocks. The shareholders of the common shares have a right to claim the company's profit and have a right to look into the decisions made by the administration. Even though the common shareholders gain a higher profit, they are also at a higher risk of losing the stocks.

Preferred Stock

In preferred stocks, the shareholders have no right to vote. The company gives the fixed dividends to the shareholders. The significant advantage of having a preferred stock is that, when the company goes bankrupt, the preferred shareholders are paid first, then the common shareholders. The corporation can even repurchase the shares from the preferred shareholders for any reason at any time.

How Are Stocks Traded?

Usually, the stock market is where a seller of the shares and a buyer meets to exchange the stocks for a specific price. As these stock markets are physical, now in this modern high-tech world, the market is growing digitally, means through the computer and internet. In other words, the stock market is becoming an electronic stock market.

It is the most common way of setting the price of the share in the auction. In this process, the sellers and buyers place certain offers and bids to sell or buy the shares. An offer is a price in which a person wants to sell the stock, whereas the bid is the price in which a person wants to buy it. When both the prices meet at the same point, a trade takes place. There are also the professional traders who make sure to continue the process of bidding and offering of the shares when the buyers and sellers do not meet.

The first step to gather stocks is to decide the purpose of your portfolio. Investors that focus on conditions for-profits, capital conservation, or capital appreciation may have exact criteria for investments.

Income-oriented investors will characteristically concentrate on low-growth businesses in industries and sectors like utilities, while other options such as REITs and master limited partnerships are also readily obtainable. Investors with low-risk hunger and mainly troubled with the defense of resources prefer to spend in safe blue-chip companies.

Bearing in mind diversification, either of the above kinds of investors could use an amalgamation of the above strategies. On the other hand, it's the simple part to decide which grouping you fall under; finding out what stocks to choose is where the procedure gets easier said than done.

Although there is no solitary correct approach to choosing stocks, a straightforward strategy will allow investors to be slender down their exploration before starting to estimate a firm's financials.

Choosing the Right Stock to Trade

You never know when the market will be in a dire shape or good shape. To capitalize on different markets, you need to find a stock that is reacting well to the market. If the market is in dire condition, you need to find the stock sliding toward a potential breakdown. You can sell it short at the right point and make big profits.

There are thousands of equities available for a trader to choose from, and day traders have no limit on the type of stocks they can trade; you can trade on virtually any stock of your choice—the stock market functions in a specific manner. Your stock can suddenly shift its direction and compels you to make extraordinary decisions, which is overall bad for your trading business. With so much electronic information at our fingerprints, it is quite easy to succumb to poor analysis. If you are applying too many chart tools to a particular stock index, you are pushing yourself into a corner.

Analyze Your Position

Stocks, just like everything else in the financial world, should be well-tailored to your goals and your financial situation. There is no singular approach while you trade in stocks. You ought to analyze first how much wealth you have that you can invest in the stock market. Write down somewhere the total capital you have and the amount that you can put on the risk. Study the market and analyze which sectors reflect your personal needs, values, and personality to conduct a discount search. Do it each day. Also, time yourself and make a head start right when the trading day opens.

Social Media

This industry is being considered as a lucrative target by day traders. Facebook and Twitter, the two giants of the social media industry, exhibit high volumes of trading in their stocks. The social media industry is the hotspot for advertisers and big business, making sure that the industry is consistently injected with big cash.

Financial Services

Financial services industries also offer great stocks for trading. For example, Bank of America is one of the most highly traded stocks per trading session. The trading volume for Bank of America is high, which makes it a liquid stock. This also applies to Morgan Stanley, Citigroup, JP Morgan & Chase, and Wells Fargo. They all have uncertain industrial conditions and high trading volumes.

Going Outside Your Geographical Boundary

When trading in the financial market, you must diversify your portfolio. Look at stocks listed in other exchanges like the London Stock Exchange (LSE) or Hong Kong's Hang Seng. Extending your portfolio outside your boundary will grant you access to potentially cheaper alternatives as well as foreign stocks.

Medium to High Instability

A day trader needs to understand the price movement to be able to make money. As a day trader, you can choose to go for stocks that typically move a lot in percentage terms or dollar terms, as these two terms usually yield different results. Stocks that typically move 3% and above every day have a consistently large intraday moves to trade. This also applies to stocks that move above $1.50 each day. Funds Available

The first instance is to take cognizance of a trader's financial position. Depending on the number of funds available, you can determine the stocks to choose from. There is a wide variety of stocks to choose from. However, you can only choose as much as your funds allow you.

Traders also need to consider buying a security in a field or industry that they are familiar with. For instance, an accountant may be happy trading financial stocks while an engineer will be at home with tech stocks, and so on. Such considerations will ensure you understand what is going on in the industry, which will boost trading ventures.

CHAPTER 15:

Advantages of Trading Scheme Leverage Options

O ptions trading is a speculative stock market trading practice where traders try to profit from any future specific stock price movements. It entails predicting the chances of a particular stock price going up in a set period and staking on its resulting future profit. When you engage in options trading, you participate in what is called financial leverage. Financial leverage refers to the concept that instead of buying the stock outright and paying the full share price amount, you can put up an initial less capital. Besides, based on the type of your options trade, you can enhance the return on your equity within or after the set time frame. Often, the amount of capital you leverage is lower than the actual share price of the stock. This apparent less capital is what gives options trading its appeal.

Advantages of Financial Leverage in Options Trading

There are two types of options, both of which have rights: call option and put option.

You will own a given number of shares as stipulated in the options contract. We call it the option contract multiplier (most options have a multiplier of x100), which means you get to own 100 shares of stock per option. Any return on your prospect is factored into this multiplier, giving you an accurate figure on your overall investment return. This multiplier is the number of shares that your option contract can be converted into if you exercised that option. You can use your right to sell your trade contract within the required time frame before the expiry date.

Your profit margins are highly magnified when compared to directly buying stocks and selling them at a profit later. In an options trading scenario, you leverage your investment at a given strike price against a future rise in the share price of that same stock price. If the stock price rises as per your speculation, the return on your investment will be much higher than direct stock trading. Your profit margin ratio is much higher, as shown by this example: Let us assume a current stock price of $20. A broker predicts the stock price to rise to $30 in a month. The trader issues a call option to buy the 20call for a $5 strike price, which expires in 1 month.

Given an option contract multiplier of 100, you can see below the marked difference in profit margin between direct stock trade of 100 shares and options trade at the specified strike price.

If the final stock price is $30 in a month:

- Direct stock trade gives you a profit of $1000, 50% of the original investment.

- Options trade gives you a profit of $500, which is 100% of the original investment.

If the final stock price is $35 in a month:

- Direct stock trade gives you a profit of $1500, which is 75% of the original investment.

- Options trade gives you a profit of $1000, which is 200% of the original investment.

Your initial cost is low. Buying options are less expensive than buying stock since it depends on the strike price at which you purchased the option. Buying stock depends on the stock price, which is usually markedly higher than the strike price. Therefore, it becomes favorable for you to buy a stake in the stock at a discounted rate.

Your call option value goes up whenever the share price rises above the stipulated initial cost.

Your put option value goes up as the share price falls below the stipulated initial cost.

You have an extra revenue stream. Profits from options trading are a source of income for your business. Given the potential for much higher returns than conventional profit revenues, it gives you the ability to engage in more ambitious business endeavors.

Financial leverage in options trading allows you to settle debts incurred in the course of business. Your business may have a margin account used to accrue debt and leverage the debt in an options contract in anticipation of receiving markedly higher returns. Once you have taken care of liabilities, options trading gives you room to invest in other business opportunities.

CHAPTER 16:

Choosing the Right Options Broker

A reference was often made to professional advice and guidance before and during any trading with options. In a few cases, it was also suggested that this advice and guidance were to be rendered by experts and not just professionals. But who are these people?

They are called options brokers, and their profession is to offer actual options trading, along with research, education, and various tools to individual investors. Apart from the above, they can also provide trade-in other financial products related to options, like stocks, funds (either mutual or exchange-traded), and bonds.

As in any profession, some good brokers and brokers do not have your best interest in their minds.

You must know if you want to deal with a regular broker or a reseller broker. The first one deals directly with you, while the latter intermediates between you and a larger broker.

If you choose a regular broker, the first thing to check is whether they belong to such an entity. If not, it would be best to avoid them.

The next choice to make is between a full-service broker and a discount broker. The full-service ones offer a lot more services, but they do not come cheap. They undertake the more significant part of the work to be done, and they will provide the professional advice and guidance required.

A discount broker may be the best choice for a beginner. For two reasons:

- The fees of a full-service one are probably not affordable for a newcomer

- You will learn more about options trading.

What usually affects the decisions on which broker to choose are the costs involved. The following will weigh a lot on your selection:

Minimum balances

To start a brokerage account, most brokers require a minimum balance. This amount ranges between $500 and $1,000.

Margin accounts

While it is not an immediate choice for beginners, it will be a significant issue as you continue trading. Margin accounts are created when the broker will lend you the money to make the trades. The securities and options that you will trade, along with the balance of your account, are held as collateral.

While it is risky (you stand to file for bankruptcy if you fail grossly), it is a handy tool to check your broker's integrity. A good broker will protest, if your choices are not sound ones, and will not lend you the money as they do not want to lose it.

Easiness of withdrawal

Just like any other professionals, brokers want to make a profit. Therefore, most of them will charge you a withdrawal fee, or will not let you close your account if the balance falls below the minimum. It is strongly recommended to make sure that you fully understand the rules about money withdrawal before you begin any cooperation with a broker.

Fee structures

Hidden fees and expenses are the greatest fear of investors. While most brokers follow similar rules, some of them have particularly complex fee structures. The less complicated the fee structure is, the better the broker.

Brokers are important, as you will not be able to start investing without a brokerage account. But keep in mind that no broker can be good at everything. So, the last issue to consider before selecting a broker is what kind of investor you are. Your broker must match with your style.

Mistakes that You Need to Avoid

As a trader, some of the mistakes you will encounter include overly aggressive positions, time decay, and unnecessary risks. However, there are other mistakes, and you must avoid these as well. Many options traders, including seasoned ones, still make these.

Problems About the Price Tag

There was advice once given never to buy something that you do not need because it is cheap. This advice is valid for a lot of things, including options positions. However, these often have a low chance of success. Avoid these kinds of mistakes. Any option that is out of the money has a long way to go before it becomes profitable. It may run out of time, and you will probably lose money. Instead, think about costlier options that are in the money. You stand a much better chance at profitability with such options.

Manage Both Greed and Fear

These emotions are primarily considered to be your worst enemy as a trader. You will notice that when a trade has a good run, a lot of investors will be greedy and will not exit the trade according to a set plan. They will try and ride the upward momentum to milk it as much as possible.

97

Greed is also evident when it comes to a downward trend. Ordinarily, traders should exit a trade when they start incurring losses. There is no need to cling to a trade believing a turnaround is just a couple of minutes away. Some traders tend to overreact and withdraw from trades the minute there is trouble. It is advisable to work out the ideal entry and exit points and then use them to take profits or count losses and then exit the trade. There is always tomorrow.

Having a plan is a basic requirement for all traders, whether amateur or experienced. Make use of the charts, examine your risk tolerance, and consider your goals as an investor. Stick to it as much as possible.

Properly Allocate Funds to Trades

You should allocate funds correctly to your trades. You do not want to allocate any amount above 5% of your investments to a single trade. Choose some trades and allocate each trade an amount between 3% and 5%. This way, you will stand to win a lot more than lose. You will also spread your risk and avoid losing all your money.

Identifying a Reliable Broker

There are lots of brokerage firms available online. These brokerage firms provide traders like you with a platform to trade safely. These firms charge you a fee to access the platform and carry out your trades. They also provide you with tools that you need to trade successfully and customer service.

The lower the fees or commission charged, the less the customer service and assistance you can expect. Anticipate paying between $2 and $5 on average per options contract that you invest in.

Sometimes you will be asked if you prefer a cash or margin account when opening an account with a broker. A cash account means you will trade using your own money. A margin account allows you access to credit facilities where you borrow money from the broker to invest in particular securities. You can only borrow money from your broker against specific securities like bonds, stocks, and mutual funds.

Options also settle trades the very same day or one business day. Therefore, you will require substantial cash amounts to enter trades. When you enter complex trades, you will also need to set some cash aside just if you are obliged to buy shares at a specific price.

CHAPTER 17:

Options for Flexible Instruments

With regards to exchanging and interest all, there is a wide range of money related instruments that can be utilized for potential benefits. A money related instrument is any tradable resource, regardless of whether it is money, proof of possession in a substance, different wares, or even the authoritative option to get or convey another budgetary instrument.

Stocks are most likely the most popular budgetary instrument, yet there are additionally bonds, prospects, and choices contracts. There is cash to be produced using putting resources into or exchanging any money related instrument.

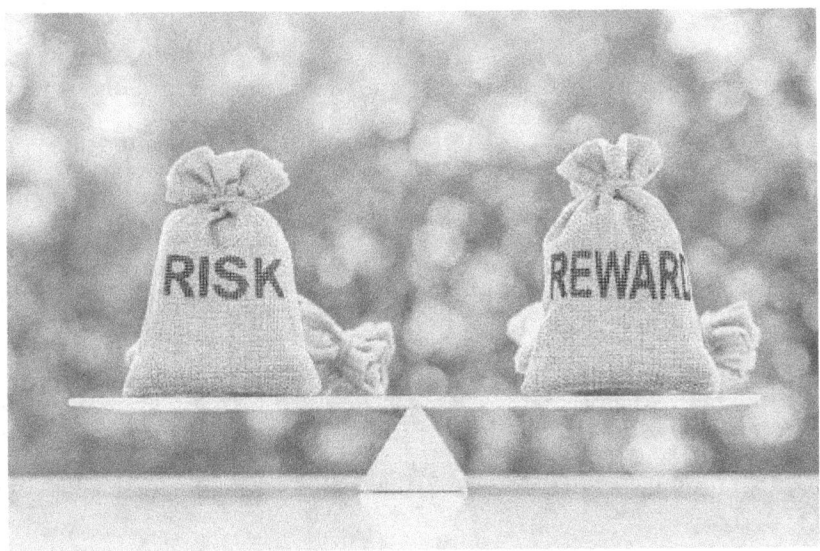

You need to recognize what choices contracts are and how they work. In any case, it likewise pays to have a comprehension of other budgetary instruments and how they work by method of examination. Regardless of whether your venture plan includes just exchanging alternatives, it can help discover more about other money-related instruments.

You may well choose to adhere to just exchanging alternatives, yet you additionally may conclude that you need to put resources into other money related instruments as well.

- Stocks

- Bonds

- Forex

- Futures

Difference Between Stocks and Options

If you somehow happened to ask how a great many people need to engage in contributing, at that point, the most widely recognized answer would likely purchase stocks in publicly recorded organizations. This is generally because purchasing stocks is probably the least difficult approach to put away cash, and anybody can do it with only a tad of information.

There is unquestionably cash to be produced using purchasing or exchanging stocks and various individuals that do precisely that. Notwithstanding, when you contrast exchanging stocks with exchanging choices, there are some unmistakable preferences that alternatives offer.

Purchasing stocks in publicly recorded organizations is one of the most widely recognized ways for individuals to put away cash. When you comprehend the rudiments in question, it's generally simple to search for appropriate speculation openings that meet your venture objectives. With the wide determination of online agents, purchasing and selling stocks is simpler than at any other time.

Numerous speculators effectively exchange stocks for making bigger returns than is conceivable. They utilize a purchase and hold technique to fabricate a portfolio that just increments in esteem after some time.

Notwithstanding, purchasing and selling stocks isn't the best way to benefit from the money related markets using any means, and numerous strategies can be utilized. Exchanging choices is one specific type of putting that has developed essentially in prevalence: among prepared, master financial specialists, however, with an entire scope of individuals.

Alternative exchanging is open to anybody. Even though it's somewhat more than simply purchasing stocks, it isn't that hard for anybody to find out about the subject and get included. One of the things you need to comprehend is how putting resources into choices is not the same as putting resources into stocks.

The principle distinction among stocks and choices is that when putting resources into stocks, you are purchasing a security that can go up or down in esteem. When putting resources into alternatives, you are purchasing a subsidiary. A subsidiary is an exchanging instrument that gets its incentive from some other security. The estimation of the subordinate is along these lines firmly connected to the estimation of that other security. This is known as the fundamental security, yet different elements can likewise influence it.

On account of alternatives, there are different protections other than stocks; it can likewise be other money related instruments, for example, items and monetary standards. There is an entire scope of various sorts of alternatives that can be purchased and sold methods you can estimate on a wide assortment of money related instruments when exchanging choices.

At the point when you purchase stocks in a specific organization, you are purchasing an offer in that organization. If the organization performs well, the odds are that your venture will increment in worth. You can decide to sell at a greater expense than you purchased to arrive at a higher benefit. Suppose the organization you have put resources into is gainful. In that case, they may grant investors a yearly profit (a portion of those benefits that is paid to any individual who holds stock in the organization).

It's conceivable to make awesome returns by holding profit paying stocks for an extended period, you despite everything, own the real resource that you can decide to sell whenever. You can likewise decide to short sell stocks in an organization and cause a benefit on the off chance that they go down in esteem.

How alternatives work is extraordinary; when you purchase investment opportunities, you are purchasing an agreement that gives you the option to purchase or sell stocks at a concurred cost. While these agreements arrive in a wide range of classifications, they would be able to be classed as either calls or puts. Calls give you the option to purchase a particular stock at a fixed value (this fixed cost is known as the strike cost) while puts give the option to sell a particular stock at a fixed cost. On the off chance that you purchase calls, the value you pay for them doesn't get you any real stock; it essentially gives you the option to get it.

So, the essential distinction between these two money related instruments is very straightforward. Purchasing stocks is paying to claim a genuine offer in an organization, while purchasing alternatives is paying for the option to purchase (or sell) shares in an organization. This distinction gives exchanging choices some noteworthy points of interest.

Favorable circumstances of Options Over Stocks

Perhaps the greatest favorable position of purchasing brings over purchasing stock is the way that you can confine potential misfortunes while still profiting by potential benefits. You should put resources into a specific organization, for instance, that had a high possibility of expanding altogether.

CHAPTER 18:

Options Trading Using Arbitrage

This kind of trading strategy focuses on capitalizing on pricing errors in two different markets trading the same or similar financial instruments. In this case, a day trader will quickly buy the financial instrument and sell it on another market to profit off the price difference in the two financial markets. This profit is made by a quick observation of the market and looking for where pricing inaccuracies exit.

While arbitrage trading is a simple way of making a profit as a day trader, you need to note these things do not happen all the time. But it is very important to look at the price of a financial instrument from the various trading markets to find where the pricing error exit and the profit from.

Institutional day traders make use of analytical software in their trading activities. This enables them to quickly track and monitor any price imbalance in the market and leverage arbitrage to make a huge amount of profit from the price differences. As an individual trader, you will stay up to date about the market and use more than the market for your trading activities.

Take an example of arbitrage trading: The stock of ABC Company sells at $11 per share on the London Stock Exchange but selling at $ 10 on the New York Stock Exchange. You quickly realize a profit from the price imbalance between two stock markets.

To profit from the price difference, you decided to buy 100 shares (total cost: ($ 1100) and then simultaneously sell them on the London York Stock Exchange (total revenue: ($ 1100). In this case, you made $ 100 from the transaction, risk-free in just a few minutes of analyzing and placing the trade.

Are Stock Options Trading Risky?

Stocks are the most unpredictable and commonly traded financial instruments in the market. Every year, millions of people trade directly in stocks. They lose their investment capital when the market goes against them. This is why trading stocks through options have been embraced by the high seasoned investor and the beginner investor.

Stock options trading provides the opportunity to invest in stocks that will generate better profits without directly risking a lot of money in the trade. While losses are limited to the amount of money used to pay for the option, many people have come to love stock options trading.

In the world of stock options, there are three most important indicators for profit: "in the money" (ITM), "out of the money" (OTM), and "at the money" (ATM). These three indicators are the main profit signals in stock options trading.

Key Tips for Stock Options Trading

Before you trade in stocks, you want to get yourself acquainted with the rules of the game. Understanding how stock options work and how to trade them will give you the edge against those who simply jump in the game without anything in mind.

You can either use put, call, or a combination of these options to trade in a market. Complex stock options strategies, such as married put, iron condor, and all others make use of a combination of call and put options.

Premium is the total money paid to purchase the underlying stock. The premium serves as an investor's incentive to take on the risk of selling the stock via the option. It generates income for the stockholder.

Every stock option, either put or call, is made up of 100 shares of stock. If you want to place a five-call option, you'll need to purchase 500 shares of the underlying stock before opening the trade.

Determine your minimum loss and maximum gains before entering the trade. This will help you avoid gambling and know whether the odds are in your favor or against you. And when you had a loss, cut your losses and move onto the next thing.

A good trading plan plus the commitment to homework are the keys to making it in stock options trading. You have to do your homework and stick to your trading plan for options trading. This is how to increase your gains.

CHAPTER 19:

How to Get Maximum Profits

You Can Profit from Any Market Situation

It is to benefit from any market situation trading options. Most options strategies are carried out by combining different option positions and sometimes even the underlying stock's position. A trading strategy can be used singly or in combination with others to profit from market situations.

You stand to make huge profits with options trading, yet your risk and exposure are limited. Ordinary stock trading does not afford you such opportunities.

The most crucial aspects of options trading know when to exit a trade and how to exit. Knowing how and when to exit is vital for successful trading.

Options strategies are the most versatile strategies in the financial markets. They provide traders and investors with numerous profit-making opportunities with limited exposure and risk.

These strategies can be favorable whether the stock price of the underlying security rises, remains the same, or falls.

Taking Profits with Options Trading

One of the best-known ways of profiting from options is through the purchase of undervalued options. You can even buy options at the right price and still benefit from them.

Options prices usually are extremely volatile. This provides an excellent chance to benefit from profit-taking. However, when you miss the right moment to take profits, you will have lost out on an amazing opportunity.

Take Advantage of Volatility and Collect Profits

Options are unlike stocks because they have a time limit. Stocks can be held indefinitely, but options can expire. This means that the time for trades is limited. As a trader, you cannot afford to miss this window. Should such a chance be missed, then it might not be seen again in a long while.

You should avoid long-term strategies when trading options. Strategies such as the average are unsuitable for options trading because of the limited time that options have. Also, watch out for margin requirements. Such requirements have to capacity to severely impact your trading funds requirements.

Watch out for multiple factors that may affect a favorable price. For instance, the price of the underlying stock may go up, which is a good thing. However, any accruing benefit may be eroded by other factors such as dividend payment, time decay, or volatility. Such constraints make it imperative that you learn to follow profit-taking strategies. Here are some of these crucial profit-taking strategies that you can use as a trader.

Trailing Stop Strategy

When using this strategy, you will set a pre-determined percentage for a particular target. For instance, you can ten options contracts with each costing $80 with a profit target at $100 and a $70 stop-loss.

Set a Profit-Taking Stop-Loss

We can set a stop-loss at 5%, which means if our target price of $100 is attained, our trailing target will be $95. If the upward trend continues and our price gets to $120, then the trailing target of 5% becomes $114. Should the price movement continue to, say, $150, then the trailing target this time becomes $142.5.

Should the price now start falling, you will exit and collect profits at this $142.5. The trailing stop lets you enjoy protection as the price increases and then exits a trade once the price turns around. The stop-loss levels should neither be too small nor too large. If they are too small, they will cause frequent triggers, whereas too large will make profit-taking unachievable.

Partial Profit Booking

Season traders have a routine that they follow to book partial profits. First, they set a target and to take profits when it is attained.

Partial profit booking helps to protect the trader's capital to a large extent. This essentially has the effect of preventing capital losses in the event of a sudden price change. Such price reversals are commonly observed in options trading.

Book Partial Profits at Regular Time Intervals

As a trader, you can book partial profits at regular time intervals. However, you will need to pay close attention to the time limit. A massive portion of your options premium is made of its time value. As time runs out, then its value also goes d. As a trader, you should keep a keen eye on the time value of your options as this erodes its value. Buyers should be careful about the time limit.

Sell Covered Call Options against Long Positions

Selling options is a lucrative income-generating process. This is not the only pathway to riches in the markets. You can also sell naked puts. This is like selling shares or stocks that you do not. When you sell naked put options, you will free up your time to do a lot more. Stock trading allows you to sell stocks of shares that you do not have for a profit. This tends to free up your capital so you can invest it or trade with it indefinitely. It is advisable to stick to stocks that you understand very well and those you would not mind. There is still hedging associated with options trading, so always be careful and watch about that. Most large investors who deal in options are often hedging.

Consider all the Options Available to You

We make assumptions that traders will hold their positions until the end. You can choose from several options to ensure that you can leverage any time you want to see its need.

Learn to Select the Right Options to Trade

You have to identify options that will see you earn a profit.

- Make sure you determine whether you are bullish or bearish on the market, sector, or just the stock. When you make these decisions, you will be able to identify the options you wish to buy.

- Consider volatility and think about how it would affect your options trading strategy. Think about the status of the market. Is it calm, or is it volatile? You may also want to consider the expiration date and strike price. If you only have a couple of shares, this would be a great time and opportunity to purchase more stock.

CHAPTER 20:

Attributes of A Successful Options Trader

A successful options trader is a unique individual. This person learns how to leverage their financial position to pave a way to profitable returns that make the time and effort invested worth it. This person is strong-willed and determined.

Even though everyone can understand these concepts and maybe the ability to implement them, not everyone dares to stick with it until they gain the results they want – which is financial freedom. A strong options trader requires a unique set of skills, attitudes, and persona.

Being self-disciplined

You may be excited about the possibility of gaining financial freedom by using options trading. If you are willing to jump with both feet in, I applaud you. I also implore you to exercise caution and, therefore, self-discipline. Do not just stop your education on options. Do more extensive research so that you can identify the best opportunities for you. Doing this will allow you to form the best strategy for your case and goals. Do not skip doing your homework because you are eager. Jumping the gun has led to many traders losing out. You need to rule your desires, wants, and actions rather than being ruled by them.

Being Committed

A successful options trader is one that does not give up. He or she does not trade on an on-again, off-again basis. This person is committed to building their financial success in this way and persists in their effort. This is something you embrace as a business and part of your lifestyle. Go hard or go home. Options trading has no room for being tentative.

Continually learning

The financial market is continuously evolving. It changes every single day. A trader needs to be able to make forecasts about the future as well. Continuously learning about the market also allows you to see new opportunities where amateur traders will not. To increase your knowledge of options is to follow an experienced options trader. The point is not to copy his or her moves. Rather, it is to watch a master at work to develop your style of trading.

Being patient

This relates to jumping the gun. Carefully weigh your options before you make a move while trading options. While there are risks involved in trading options, the market typically provides signs of these opportunities if a trader knows where and how to look. Control your emotions and strategize your entry into the trade market as well as your exit from trades.

Being an effective risk manager

There is no guarantee when you trade options. An effective options trader needs to be able to exploit his or her position to determine where he or she should take appropriate measures to capitalize on his or her gain. Part of managing risks involves diversifying your portfolio so that all your eggs are not in one basket. A successful trader does not go chasing after every available option. Managing risks significantly lowers the chances of loss happening effectively.

Being able to manage money effectively

A trader needs to know how much capital should be allocated for trading. Throwing your money at all options will not lead to effective results. This is a recipe for losing money. Part of being a good money manager means that the trader needs to be good with numbers so that he or she can calculate the Vega, theta, delta, and gamma of their trade options.

Being an effective planner

While there is a level of relying on instinct in trading options, you also need to have a plan, so you do not place random trades. You need to have a direction to effectively move forward with obtaining financial freedom no matter which option you choose. Having smart goals allow you to develop this plan. You also need to have a plan to cover any losses that may happen and a plan for how you can leverage the profit that you do make. Your plan needs to allow for flexibility, and the great thing is that you can upgrade, downscale, and change the plan completely if need be.

Being able to accept losses gracefully

The nature of the financial market is unpredictable, and every trader makes a loss at some point. Having an apt understanding of the market will minimize this loss, but you also need to be flexible in handling this so that you do not get blindsided or let this weigh you down. Remember that any successful person needs to be able to find a lesson in their failure to be better in the future.

CHAPTER 21:

Ways to Improve Your Options Trading

O ptions fall among the most flexible trading gadgets on the monetary marketplace today. They allow investors to make cash from the downside, upside, and sideways movement of the market. There has continuously been a myth that options trading is both volatile and complicated. It is simple to look options as something robust to alternate in. However, this isn't always true. Only that the use of options as a trading instrument involves numerous dangers, much like any other instrument, not all people come out a hit. However, anyone with exact primary data about options can efficiently make it inside the marketplace.

Most hit investors have guidelines and tricks that they appoint to make sure they make a few good profit trading options. Here are a number of them.

Understand Technical and Fundamental Analysis

Before you start trading, make sure that you perform an analysis of the marketplace. The technical evaluation includes the study of the way the charge is anticipated to sell.

Fundamental evaluation, on the opposite hand, facilitates you to research social, economic, and political elements that may additionally affect the demand and supply of the stock you desire to trade-in. Amount and call for the effect the rate of trade can be used to detect the course of stock costs easily. In a nutshell, technical, and essential evaluation of the market helps you to identify similar patterns round the rate and make knowledgeable options on your options.

Have Enough Capital

The cause why most novices do now not make it in options trading is not having sufficient capital. Most people get excited at how secure options trading may be and assume that they could make an instant benefit from their little money in a depend on days. However, earlier than they recognize it, some trades have swallowed their capital. They are then left with nothing to trade on. To be on the secure side, start with a significant amount of money to sustain you for several trades.

What differentiates investors is their preferences, personalities, and trading styles. You want to apprehend the fashion that fits you first-rate. For example, a few buyers decide to work at night while others are extra effective in day trading. Some of the investors will make several short sales at some stage in the day at the same time as others will component in the issue of time and volatility simply to benefit massive earnings over periods that can also close among few days and a month.

Learn from your losses and use the statistics to make better trades. You want a whole lot of time to exercise on business earlier than engaging in the actual activity.

Back-test Your Trading Strategy

Back-testing is a very critical component, while it comes to developing a winning plan. It includes comparing your existing strategy and fashion against the market history to peer how exceptional you will carry out. Although past overall performance does now not necessarily decide destiny success, doing this will provide you with a rough image of how your strategy and fashion may additionally carry out at different times and set-ups. In case you are unable to do that by yourself, you may engage a software business enterprise or Forex broking to do the again trying out for you.

One benefit of returned-checking out is that it enables you to perceive areas inside your approach that want to be improved. For the system to be accurate, you want to take into account a few elements:

- Ensure the period is accurate. It is recommended that you check an approach over long durations of time than brief ones. This is because long intervals frequently produce precise outcomes.

- Stick to at least one sector. If your method is constrained on options trading, your lower back-check should only receive recognition on options trading.

- Do not use results to make conclusive options. In most cases, beyond performances might not always reflect what happens within the future. As a lot as back-trying out can also depict your approach as a notable one, it is right to go away room for possible failure or underperformance of the

Create a Risk Management Plan

When it comes to options trading, do not invest any money which you are can't manage to pay for to lose. Before sealing an agreement, think about the worst-case state of affairs in phrases of what you can suffer from the transaction and if you'll be able to endure the loss. Beginners always have a hassle getting over a loss. To help you remain on the safe side, do now not positioned massive possibilities of your capital in an unmarried alternate. Always break up your capital into bits, spare some money in a hobby producing account, then use the relaxation for trading. This ensures which you do now not lose all your capital in options trading.

Having a plan is critical in your success. You want to have it in the area before you begin trading. Remember, options are high-risk tools, and it is essential to have strategies in a location that allow you to reduce the dangers involved with each trade. Use your cash wisely. Diversify the stocks you trade in to reduce the potential of losing all of your capital. Most professional investors most effectively seal a contract while there are a low danger and excessive profits.

Be Patient and Disciplined

To be triumphant in options trading, you must broaden a great feel of the area. Carry out significant research and set the right dreams. Stick to these desires and have them in thoughts as you seize trading opportunities. Be careful not to follow the group and don't believe in a few records and critiques earlier than perform some studies. In other words, have an approach this is impartial of outside influences. This does no longer mean which you forget about boards that provide you with beneficial records about options trading and the economic market at big. Just make sure to observe the tendencies, learn from the market, and make useful trades primarily based on your findings.

Patience will help you get the right opportunity to make an income. Expert traders can live idle for days, only looking at the marketplace and ready for a great time to prepare or near a sale. Impatient buyers will constantly whine on fewer earnings or significant losses. Wait for the odds to work in you want and cognizance on the larger photo.

Patience and field will help you persist with your capital and chance management plans. These attributes also help you to avoid trades you are not a hit in.

Understand the Market Cycle

The options trading marketplace keeps changing every time. You need to stay up to date in the marketplace traits and make the necessary changes to your plan accordingly. Through consistent studying, you will be able to examine new techniques and pick out better trading possibilities that every other investor bypass.

Understand while to alternate and when to exit. Know while the market is taking an uptrend or declining. Follow and interpret Forex news to understand what to expect in the future and the industry heading.

Keep Records

Having a past trades file helps you determine while making a name or positioned alternative efficaciously. Some of the hit traders maintain facts of all their transactions. Analyzing these statistics lets you identify essential styles in the options you're trading in. It can also assist in enhancing your odds in the alternate.

As you look at the information, be sure to keep some degree of flexibility, relying on your overall performance on each marketplace. Learn a way to exit a market that isn't always operating in your desire. You also have to be given any losses incurred because this form a part of each studying process. Options trading regularly offers with numbers so that you ought to be correct at making beneficial calculations.

Conclusion

Trading options involves a selection of considerations both before as well as after the trade have been placed. Many of the mistakes mentioned may be accounted for before the trade is opened through the use of the tools and materials. The one most significant step to trading options is developing a scheme as well as stick with it! Several of the equipment, as well as materials that will help you build your plan. Make use of these along with other trading programs and resources Fidelity offers to allow you to stay away from these typical choices trading mistakes in the future trades of yours.

Once again, day trading is not for everybody. However, based upon hard-won, individual experience, provides you with the details you require to see if day trading is an excellent individual option for you on your journey to monetary liberty and security.

It offers you the type of standard detailed details you've been trying to find to make an educated choice about day trading. Make no error about it; this kind of speculative stock trading is not for everybody. By setting out the procedure you require to go through in a practical and useful method, you get a clear concept of precisely what you'll be entering when you begin day trading.

Far from dissuading or downhearted, it also provides a practical and well-balanced view of what it's like to prepare to trade, in addition to the truths you'll deal with when you day trade. You get vital pointers on the state of minds you require to embrace, the tools you need to get, crucial strategies effective and reliable day traders utilize, and directions on how to establish your extremely own effective individual day-trading method.

You are looking at the best manuscript if you are a total rookie to day trading and desire the within dope or straight talk about this kind of securities trading. Rather of investing an excessive quantity of time and volume area on just how much you can make from day trading, in addition to the monetary liberty you can delight in, this manuscript focuses the majority of its firepower on what you require to understand so you can be successful with day trading.

One of my favorite things about options is that you can get involved in options trading without having money very much. If people were smart and disciplined about it, options trading could even provide a way out of a low-income situation. You can start trading with a hundred dollars, and if you are careful with it a year from now, there is no reason that you could not significantly grow that into a large trading account.

Just remember that options trading is a serious business, but it can be fun and exciting too. There is no reason why making money has to be tedious and difficult. You can get involved at the highest levels of our economy with the best companies by trading options. You will be able to go by on the stock market and earn some of your profits.

ANDREW CAYMAN

OPTIONS AND DAY TRADING:

Everything You Need To Know To Make Money Online. Start Investing In Options, Stocks And Futures Like An Expert Trader.

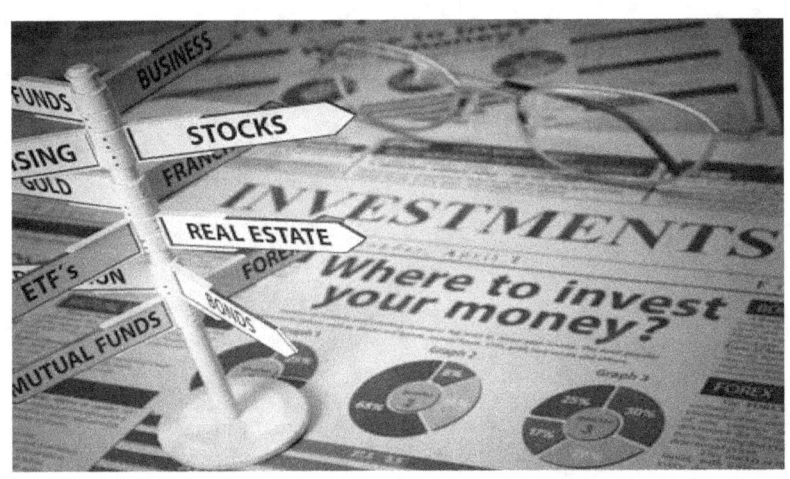

Table of Contents

Introduction

There are a lot of benefits with day trading. Everyone can profit from this kind of trading, as long as they are willing to take some time to look through the trends and charts and make sound decisions. You also need to be willing to leave your emotions at the door. While day trading can be profitable and a lot of fun, many times, it can be challenging and emotional as well, especially if a trade starts to go against what you were hoping to see.

There are a ton of securities and stocks on the market that you can choose from. It provides you with many opportunities to enter the market and provides you with some freedom when it comes to seeing results. And if you want to add in some variety to the trading, you can pick out different security to work with for that day.

You aren't restricted to just working with the stock market. Even though this is the most common place to work with trading, it isn't the only option available for you to choose from. You can someday trade with the Forex market, futures, options, cryptocurrencies, and the stock market.

Even though you will only stay in the market for a short amount of time with day trading, there are still a ton of strategies that you can choose to work with. These strategies allow you to work on different securities and market conditions. With day trading, you can do well with your trading regardless of what the market may be doing from one day to the other.

A lot of people like about day trading because it provides a huge potential for rewards. Many day traders are successful throughout the world, and they use their experience and their research to earn some big returns on every trade. Even beginners can see some great results as long as they are willing to learn and pay attention to the market. The highest rewards are some of the biggest reasons that so many people choose to get started with day trading.

Day trading provides you with the potential to earn an income from home each day, as long as you pick the right securities and the right strategies. It can take months or more to make any significant amount of money when it comes to long-term trades. The fact that you can make a good income from home each day is another reason some people love working with day trading.

With other forms of investing, you will hold onto your position overnight. There is always some risk of holding the position overnight because you never know when the price is going to drop and start lower the following day, and there is nothing you can do to prevent this when you are asleep. Day trading is going to get rid of this risk because you will exit the trade the night before, and never worries about your position going down in value. You need to know about the trading world and have a good idea about your risk tolerance, enough capital on hand, and realistic goals before you can get started with this as a viable career choice.

Remember that by reading this book, you will learn the option benefits you can enjoy when trading. This will help traders to know the market, resources, and how to work on different strategies. You don't have to apply everything you have learned at the same time. Take small steps every day and practice the strategies and tips to be a successful trader.

CHAPTER 22:

Options Basics

Options are a popular instrument that is used in the stock market. It is a great choice for beginners, as it will help them understand how the stock market works.

What are Options?

Options are security instruments that are easy to trade in. You do not have to go the lengths that you have to trade in stocks and can easily buy and sell options. Many types' of securities can be traded as options. The underlying security should be stated when you get into the deal so that you can do research on the same.

Types of Options?

Options can be of two main types, American options, and European options. You must understand these in order to deal with them.

American Options

American options refer to those that can be exchanged at any time even before the maturity or the expiry date of the options. Say for example you bought an option in May 2016 and it will mature in May 2017. If in December, you have the chance to sell the option and attain a profit from it then you can sell it freely. These form the most issued types of options.

European Options

These form the other types of options that are issued. European options unlike American options will not allow you to sell them any time. You must wait until they mature in order to do so. Even if it proves to be a good option to sell them in between, you will not be able to do so. This type is not popular anymore and is generally avoided by most traders.

Note that these are just names of the options and have no geographic relevance.

Concepts of Options

These are the different concepts of options.

Call option

The call option refers to the option to buy assets at an agreed price on or prior to a date. The date is agreed upon by the buyer and the seller. Generally, the seller has a say in it, as he will be looking to profit from the deal. During the same period, the buyer will hope for the price to rise so that he can get a good deal out of it.

Put option

The put option is the opposite of the call option. It refers to the option to sell certain assets at an agreed price on a chosen date. Here, the seller will hope for the price of the stock to drop so that the buyer will refuse to buy it and he will be left with the money paid as advance.

Trading Option Benefits

Easy to understand

The very first advantage of options is that the concept is easy to understand, and you can start investing in it at the earliest. You can go through the meaning and concepts again to understand it better. Many youngsters find it easy to start trading in options and prefer it to the other types of stock market investments.

Flexibility

Options, as you know, allow you to remain flexible. You can either buy the option or refuse to do so. You have enough time to think about the deal and can walk away from it if you think the deal is not a good idea. This flexibility is what appeals to many investors as they have the chance to prevent their hands from getting burnt. You can also extend the time in some cases if you wish to conduct some more research on the topic.

Low Risk

There is a sense of low risk that is attached to options. This is mainly because you have the chance to know if or not a particular deal will work for you. You have to take time out to study the deal and see if it is lucrative. Only then should you go ahead with it. The risk factor will always count when you are investing a lot of money into it and dealing with it on a daily basis.

High Returns

The options market has the capacity to leave you with big returns. You will be able to control a lot of money with just a small investment. There are stories of how people have made thousands of dollars with just a small investment. How much you invest in it is completely up to you. But even with a small initial investment you will be able to gain a lot from your options.

Many options

As you know, there are many underlying securities in the options markets. You can look for particular securities to invest in like say just stocks or just foreign investments. The choice is yours and you can choose something that will work best for you. But remember to diversify it and choose different options.

Trading Options Disadvantages

Risk

As you know, there are certain risks associated with trading in options. You have to exercise precaution and must not go all out at investing in a big way. The more precaution that you practice, the better it is for you. Try to understand everything that there is to about options first and only then should you invest with it. The risks involved will intensify because it is day trading. You have to remain alert and do as is right for you.

Low liquidity

You have to understand that options will have low liquidity. This means that they cannot be easily sold in the market. If you offer any of the underlying securities to the people in the market, then they might be a little apprehensive and find it tough to buy it from you. Even if it is a good security, they might still have their doubts about it. You have to sell it to them in such a way that they are convinced of its actual value. That can pose a challenge. The risk of illiquidity is what chases away many but if you understand how to sell options then you will not find it difficult.

Time lapse

One danger is that the options might take a little too much time to change in value. Maybe they will rise in value just a day after you refuse them owing to a fall in their prices. It is a little hard to predict the direction that these securities will take. You have to indulge in understanding the different prediction techniques if you wish to know whether or not the securities will do well. If you find it tough to do so, then you can take the help of a friend who is well versed in it. Don't make the mistake of getting into something that you don't know works or not. Even if you do, tell yourself that it is a learning curve.

Information

There can be some spurious information out there, which might throw you off and confuse you. If you are receiving any emails from sources that you cannot identify, then it is best that you do not entertain them at all. Turn a blind eye to it and continue with your trading. Many rookies make the mistake of believing what they see on the Internet, news or emails. They assume that they are reading what is good information and end up making investment mistakes. You surely don't want that happening to you, especially if you are just starting out.

Not for all securities

Remember that the options market is not open to all types of securities. There are only certain types like stocks, ETFs etc. So, if you are looking for something very specific then you might not find it in the options market. However, that is a good thing for some as the options reduce and you will not have to go through a lot of details to find the best one for yourself. Many times, people make the mistake of having a lot of options and then choose the wrong one. That will be successfully eliminated if you wish to trade with options.

Chapter Summary

Options are security instruments that are easy to trade in and popular instrument that is used in the stock market. It is a great choice for beginners, as it will help them understand how the stock market works. You do not have to go the lengths that you have to trade in stocks and can easily buy and sell options.

Options can be of two main types, American options, and European options. You must understand these in order to deal with them.

- American Options

- European Options

These are the different concepts of options.

- Call option

- Put option

Trading Option Benefits

- Easy to understand

- Flexibility

- Low Risk

- High Returns

Disadvantages

- Risk

- Low liquidity

- Time lapse

- Information

- Not for all securities

CHAPTER 23:

Day Trading Options Basics

The options trading approach has more than one way. If you want to get in the thick of things, then being an options day trader is the right path for you.

What Options Day Traders Do

When a trader gets into trading, they are hopeful that everything will play out well and that they will start making a lot of profits in no time. To succeed in trading, a trader must know what trade all is about.

This means that they should fully be aware of the strategies in trading, risks involved, how to manage the risks, and, importantly, understand the psychology involved in the trade.

Trading involves you invest your money into the investment. It is essential for a beginner trader to fully understand the business before investing in large sums of money.

It is vital that as a trader, you understand how to stick to your methods no matter how tempting it gets. Sticking to your strategy shows that you trust your understanding of the market and cannot easily quit.

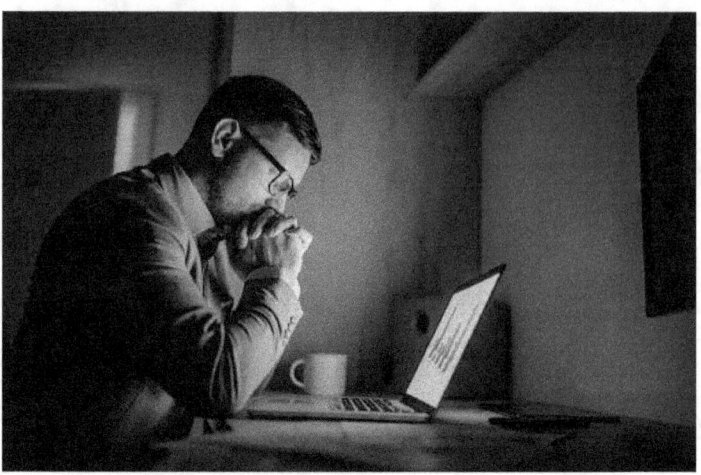

How to Get Started

The first thing to consider when getting started in day trading, is which market you want to use to trade. The important thing to recognize with day trading is that day traders routinely have strings of losses. Day trading isn't a hobby or a game. It's a serious business, and just like any serious business day, trading will require a serious commitment even before you get started.

Choose a broker

If you are already investing in stocks independently outside an employer or a mutual fund you may already have a broker that can also act as a broker for day trading purposes. Top brokers that retail investors can use include Ally Bank, TD Ameritrade, Trade Station, Interactive Brokers, ETrade, Charles Schwab, and many others.

Trading on the Stock Market

Experts advise that you need to have at least $25,000 in the capital that you can risk day trading to trade on the stock market. Making four trades in a week will qualify as being a day trader. If you plan to day trade four days per week, it's recommended that you have $30,000, to give yourself a bit of a buffer over the minimum. However, this value is quoted as assuming that you're going to be trading actual shares of stock. It is recommended that your maximum risk on trade be limited to 1% of your total capital.

It's important to know your risk and position risk. Position risk is the number of shares times the risk. Stocks with higher volatility will require more risk than stocks with lower volatility. A good way to get in on day trading on the stock market is by trading options. Buying an options contract only requires that you invest in the premium. Trading in options lets you leverage your money.

Futures Markets

You can day trade on futures markets with less capital. This can still let you get involved with stocks, however. For example, you can day trade the S&P 500 on the futures markets with a fraction of the capital required for day trading stocks. You can probably get started on this for between $1,000-$2,500. The daily range of futures can run from 10-40 points depending on volatility.

FOREX Markets

Forex markets are the lowest priced opportunity, with an entry level of capital of about $500. If you are interested in getting into day trading but lack capital, the FOREX markets can be considered to get started with day trading. Even though FOREX markets have smaller required minimum accounts, the same rules apply. Traders should not risk more than 1% of their capital on a single trade.

Planning for Success

Good traders make plans before every trade they enter to ensure that they are always making the best possible moves in the market. Great traders do not just make plans; they validate them against their notes, additional research, and other people's experiences to ensure that they have the best plans possible. Great traders know that getting involved in a trade deal can be stressful, and they want access to the best possible strategy before they go in so that they can execute their trades to the highest profits possible.

Remember that you never want to pivot or change a strategy once you are invested in a trade, so you need to make sure that you have the best strategy before going into your trade. This means you need to have your risk tolerance and maximum loss identified and validated as being a strong position, and you need to have your target profit made so that you know when to exit the market with your profits. You also need to outline how and when you will manage the trade, so you know exactly how often to check-in without being obsessive or unnecessarily stirring up stress inside yourself.

Your Goals

Understand your trading goals, as this will help you push on when the market doesn't seem to be working out well for you. The primary purpose of trading is to get money, but you should have a reason for why you need the money. Having the exact reason in your mind why you need the money will keep you more motivated to be a better trader every day. A clear objective will make you want to keep going even when you feel like giving up. You need to have stringent goals for yourself. Goals will assist you in working towards something that you need to accomplish. Visualize your goals so good and perform day trading towards them. Work hard and you will succeed in day trading.

Personal Development

Immediately when you start trading. You must identify your weaknesses. The earlier you learn about your shortcomings, the quicker you get to work on it before you are exposed to losing money. You will get to know if the weaknesses are something you could work on yourself or need help from other experienced traders. It is good to try working by yourself first since then, which means that you get to learn your weaknesses further. When this doesn't work out, then it is good to seek help from other traders.

Identifying your strength is essential as it will help you stop wasting time when you can follow your strengths to achieve an intended trade goal. Every trader is different; what one trader finds to be their weakness could be another trader's strength and vice versa. The trick is to identify what will do for you as a trader. The trader has to find out where they are going wrong and amend or replace the mistakes for better trading experiences.

Developing a Time Schedule

Have a schedule for your trading. Do not rush to trade immediately when the market opens. These are risky moments since the trades might be of the nights, and the market is not stable. You should know the best time to make your trade. Different market securities have a different time to trade. Do not be overexcited and do things anyhow. Have a timing plan for your trades.

Allow yourself time to adapt to the market, to know how trading works, and even understand the many risks you are likely to incur. Allowing yourself time to just adjust to the market without so much greed for the money will make you a great trader who will succeed in the long run.

Entry into the Options Trading Market

To survive in this game, you ought to know the entry plus that of exit prices. Day trading, like any other business, has worst-case scenarios. The entry price will help you understand when to get in while the exit point will help you know when to get out. With the prices, you will able to plan yourself on how to handle things in terms of market disasters with no worries.

The Qualities of an Effective Options Day Trader

Be Focused

Being focused will save you from lots of trouble. If you want to be successful, get yourself together and have strategies and plans on trading. Know when the right time is to make trades so as not to miss the golden time to do your trades.

Disciplined

Discipline is actually what it takes to be a successful day trader. Develop strict rules and don't trust emotions. Day traders can also use technical analysis.

Learn from Others

When you are trading, everyone else who is involved in trades is considered your competition. All of these people invest in the same market as you and behave in ways that you hope will result in you being able to take advantage of positions that will earn you more profits.

Consistent Research

One way that experienced traders manage to increase their skill level and become expert traders is through consistently engaging in informative research. Experienced traders never assume that they know everything, even if they have been successfully trading stocks for years. They know that patterns are always changing, the market is always evolving, and there is no way that they could ever know everything that there is to know about trading on the stock market.

Chapter Summary

A trader must know what trade all is about to succeed in trading. This means that they should fully be aware of the strategies in trading, risks involved, how to manage the risks, and, importantly, understand the psychology involved in the trade.

The first thing to consider when getting started in day trading, is which market you want to use to trade what broker to use.

- Trading on the Stock Market

- Futures Markets

- FOREX Markets

Planning for Success

Good traders make plans before every trade they enter to ensure that they are always making the best possible moves in the market.

Your Goals

Understand your trading goals, as this will help you push on when the market doesn't seem to be working out well for you. Goals will assist you in working towards something that you need to accomplish.

Personal Development

You must identify your weaknesses to learn your shortcomings and identifying your strength is essential as it will help you stop wasting time when you can follow your strengths to achieve an intended trade goal.

Developing a Time Schedule

Do not rush to trade immediately when the market opens. Allow yourself time to adapt to the market, to know how trading works, and even understand the many risks you are likely to incur.

Entry into the Options Trading Market

The entry price will help you understand when to get in while the exit point will help you know when to get out.

The Qualities of an Effective Options Day Trader

- Be Focused

- Disciplined

- Learn from Others

- Consistent Research

CHAPTER 24:

The Trading Market

U nderstanding the market trends gives the trader an upper hand as they know when to buy and when to sell their securities. A day trader should have sufficient market knowledge. Failing to study and understand the market will only make you fail in your day trading activity. It is imperative to understand the securities that are worth buying and those that you should stay away from.

Deciding What Market to Trade In

You have to consider several things when choosing your trading market. One of the most important factors is your financial position. If you can't afford to start trading $30,000, you'll have to skip the stock market and settle for the futures, cryptocurrency, or foreign exchange markets instead.

A trading system is required for a day trade. If you don't have the necessary equipment or software to day trade, you'll be very hard-pressed to succeed in day trading

Consider also the time zone. The United States isn't the only day trading market that can provide profit opportunities. There are other day trading markets around the world, i.e., different time zones. If you're a night owl, maybe financial markets from the other side of the pond may be more suited for you. If you're a day person, you shouldn't have a problem trading the United States markets.

Your personality and interests may also play essential roles in your ability to day trade successfully in specific markets.

When you have finally chosen your starting market, commit to sticking to it for the foreseeable future. Flipping back and forth between different markets isn't just stressful, but it can also impede your ability to master a particular market. Focus is the key.

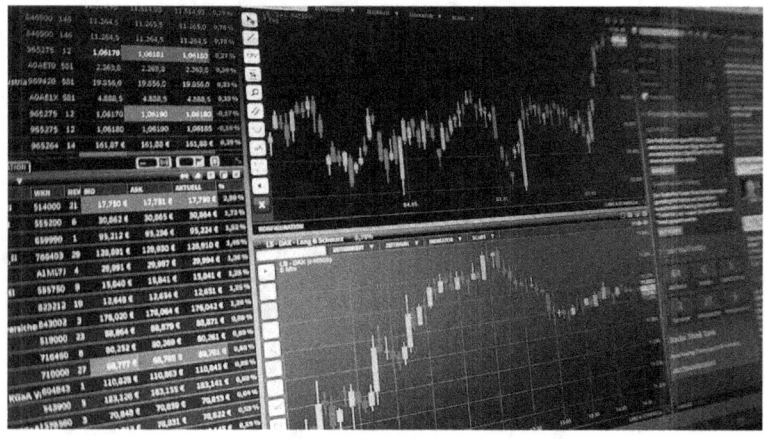

How to Find the Best Options to Day Trade

If you'd like to start day trading in the United States' stock market, you'll need a minimum of $25,000 in your broker's account at all times. This means if your equity balance falls below this amount at any point, your day trading privileges may be suspended until you put in more money to meet the minimum amount. Your equity balance includes your cash balance and the current market value of the stocks you're holding.

Considering the highly volatile nature of day trades, you'll be better off starting with an equity balance higher than the minimum. Another popular day trading market is the futures market. As the name implies, this is the market to trade futures contracts, which are nothing more than formal agreements to buy or sell a specific number or amount of particular assets at a fixed price, regardless of what the price of such assets is in the future.

Day traders can make money day trading futures the same way they do with stocks, i.e., they buy futures contracts at a lower price and sell them at a higher price within the same trading day. Trading hours for futures markets aren't as fixed as those in the stock market. They depend on the kind of contracts involved. Pay close attention to the trading day's actual end for the type of contracts you're trading to avoid carrying an open position to the next one.

Once you start day trading, you can use several techniques and methods to execute trades. You can choose to trade based solely on your gut feeling. You can go to the other extreme of relying entirely on mathematical models that optimize trading success through elaborate automated trading systems. Regardless of the method, you can have limitless day-trading profit potential once you master day trading.

Technical Analysis

Indicators and charts are one of the essential components of technical analysis. It can represent different information and may appear in various forms. In the graphical analysis, the graphs deserve particular attention because they represent a given financial instrument's price dynamics and in a given period.

The analysis of the graphs is for particular shapes, also called graphic structures, configurations, figures. They are figures that emerge from the price movement, and that can signal its future trend. They are tracked by analysts joining points in the price graph of financial security or an indicator's performance. The purpose is to identify the most typical price patterns for forecasting.

Price Charts

Charts are used by traders to monitor price changes. These changes determine when to enter or exit a trading position. There are several charts used in day trading. Although these charts differ in functionality and layout, they typically offer the same information to day traders.

159

Line Charts

These are very popular in all kinds of stock trading. They do not give the opening price, just the closing price. You are expected to specify the chart's trading period to display the closing price for that period. The chart creates a line that connects closing prices for different periods using a line.

Most days, traders use this chart to establish how a security price has performed over different periods. However, you cannot rely on this chart as the only information provider when it comes to making some critical trading decisions. This is because the chart only gives you the closing price. This means that you may not establish other vital factors that have contributed to the current changes in the price.

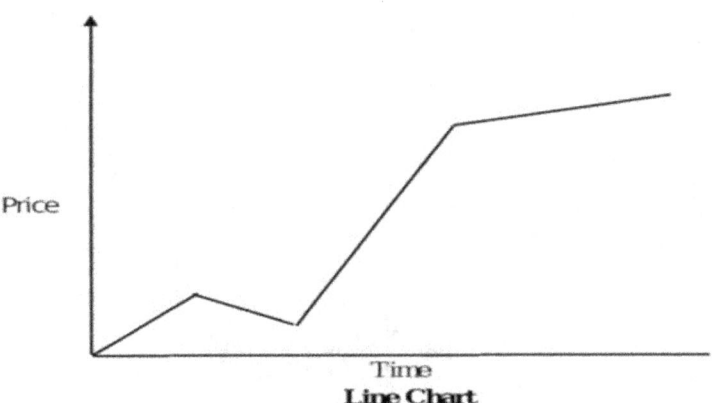

Line Chart

Open-Hight- Low-Close Bar Chart

These are lines used to indicate price ranges for a particular stock over time. Bar charts comprise vertical and horizontal lines. The horizontal lines often represent the opening and closing costs. The horizontal line is always black if the closing price is higher than the opening price. When the opening price is higher, the line becomes red.

Bar charts offer more information than line charts. They indicate opening prices, the highest and lowest prices as well as the closing prices. They are always easy to read and interpret. Each bar represents rice information. The vertical lines indicate the highest and lowest prices attained by a particular stock. The opening price of a stock is always shown using a small horizontal line on each vertical line's left. The closing price is a small horizontal line on the right.

When the vertical lines are long, it shows that there is a significant difference between the highest price attained by security and the lowest price. Therefore, large vertical lines indicate that the commodity is highly volatile, while small lines indicate slight price changes. When the closing price is far much higher than the opening price, it means that the buyers were more during the stated period.

Bar chart information is always differentiated using color codes. Therefore, you must understand what each color means, as this will help you know whether the price is going up or down.

OHLC Bar Charts!

Sellers firmly in control

Sellers lose commitment

Sellers lose control to buyers

Candlesticks Chart

Candlestick charts are used on almost every trading platform. These charts carry a lot of information about the stock market and stock prices. They help you get information about the opening, closing, highest, and lowest stock prices.

The opening price is always indicated as the first bar on the left of the chart, and the closing price is on the chart's far-right. Besides these prices, the candlestick chart also contains the body and wick.

These are the features that differentiate the candlestick for other day trading charts.

One great advantage of candlestick charts entails using different visual aspects when indicating the closing, opening, highest, and lowest stock prices. These charts compute stock prices across different time frames. Each chart consists of three segments:

- The upper shadow

- The body

- The lower shadow

The body of the chart is often red or green. Each candlestick is an illustration of time. The data in the candlestick represents the number of trades completed within the specified time.

The high point represents the highest stock price while low stands for the lowest price of a stock.

The candlestick's body will be red when the closing price is lower than the opening price. If the closing price is higher, the body will be colored green.

Factors That Affect Options Market

There are different options markets available. Options can be based on a variety of securities. Different traders have different needs and variations when it comes to options contracts. There are also various reasons why traders choose to deal in options rather than other financial instruments. There are a few factors that affect the options market.

Strike Price:

This is the price that you will sell or buy the underlying stock should you choose to exercise your options. Also called the exercise price.

Expiration Date:

The options contract is not indefinite and has an expiration date. The expiration date referred to the time when the contract entered into becomes void or expires.

Premium:

This term refers to the price you pay for the option. This price is charged per share, which means it will depend on the number of shares you sign up to. Premium has different components to it. These are the intrinsic value and time value of an option.

Intrinsic Value:

This is the value of an option and refers to the difference between the underlying stock's strike price and its current market price.

Time value:

The time value of a share refers to the amount of time available before an options contract expires. The time value decreases as the expiry date approaches. Time decay is the term used to express the approach of the expiration date. As this time decay progresses, the time value of an option decreases. This time is derived from the pricing model that was used to calculate it. Time is precious to investors hence the importance of time decay.

Chapter Summary

A day trader should have sufficient market knowledge to know when to buy and sell their securities. It is imperative to understand the securities that are worth buying and those that you should stay away from. You can use several techniques and methods to execute trades once you start day trading. You can have limitless day-trading profit potential once you master day trading regardless of the method.

Indicators and charts represent different information and may appear in various forms. The graphs deserve particular attention because they represent a given financial instrument's price dynamics and in a given period. Charts are used by traders to monitor price changes. These changes determine when to enter or exit a trading position. There are several charts used in day trading. Although these charts differ in functionality and layout, they typically offer the same information to day traders.

- Line Charts

- Open-Hight- Low-Close Bar Chart

- Candlesticks Chart

Factors that affect the options market are stock price, expiration date, premium, intrinsic value, and time value.

CHAPTER 25:

Options Day Trading Styles

N o matter what style or strategy an options day trader chooses to use, there are three essential components. These elements are:

Liquidity

This factor describes how quickly an option or other asset can be bought and sold without affecting the current market price. Liquid options are more desirable to an options day trader because they trade easier. It creates more resistance in the ease at which a trader can open or close their position. It expands the time needed to complete the transactions involved and can lead to a loss for the options day trader.

Volatility

This describes how sensitive the assets attached to the options are to price changes due to external factors. Some assets are more volatile than others. Stocks and cryptocurrencies are volatile assets. Volatility has a high impact on an options day trader's profit margin.

Volume

This describes the number of options being traded at a specific time interval. Volume indicates the associated assets price movement on the market because it is a gage of the asset's interest in the market. The higher the volume, the more desirable traders typically are in pursuing an option. Volume is one of the factors that make up open interest.

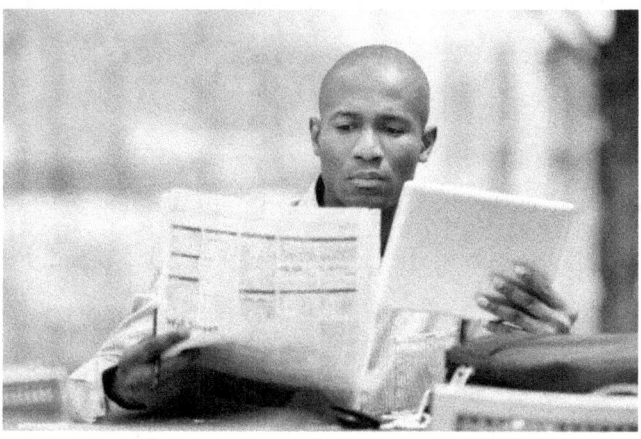

Breakout Options Day Trading

Breakout describes the process of entering the market when prices move out of their typical price range. For this style of trading to be successful, there needs to be an accompanying increase in volume. There is more than one type of breakout, but we will discuss one of the most popular support and resistance breakouts. The support and resistance method describe how the associated asset price stops decreasing (support) and the point at which the related asset price stops increasing (resistance). The day trader will enter a long position if the associated asset price breaks above resistance. On the other hand, the options day trader will enter a short position if the associated asset breaks below the supported price. As you can see, the trader's position depends on if the asset is supported or resisted at that new price level. As the asset transcends the normal price barrier, volatility typically increases. This usually results in the price of the associated asset moving in the direction of the breakout. The day trader will take on a bearish position if this price is said to be above the resistance level. A bullish approach is a typical maneuver if prices are set to close below the support. Exit strategies require a more sophisticated approach. The options day trader needs to consider past performance and use chart patterns to determine a price target to close their position. Once the goal has been reached, the day trader can exit the trade and enjoy its profit.

Momentum Options Day Trading

This options day trading style describes the process of options day trading relying on price volatility and the rate of change of volume. It is so-called because the main idea behind the strategy is that the force behind the associated asset's price movement is enough to sustain it in the same direction. This is because when an asset increases in price, it typically attracts investors, which drives the price even higher. Options day traders who use this style ride that momentum and profit from the expected price movement. This analysis gives the day trader an overall picture that includes momentum indicators like:

- The momentum indicator, which makes use of the most recent closing price of the associated asset to determine the strength of the price movement as a trend.

- The relative strength index (RSI), which is a comparison of profits and losses over a set period.

- Moving averages, which allows the day trader to see passed fluctuations to analyze the market trends.

- The stochastic oscillator, which compares the most recent closing prices of the associated asset over a specified time.

Momentum options day trading is highly effective and simple as long as it is done right. The day trader needs to keep abreast of the news and earnings reports to make informed decisions using this trading style.

Reversal Options Day Trading

This style relies on trading against the trend and the opposite of momentum options day trading. Also called trend trading or pull back trending, it is performed when an options day trader can identify pullbacks against the current price movement trends. It can be quite profitable when the trade goes according to plan. Because of the depth of market knowledge and trading experience needed to perform this style effectively, it is not recommended for beginners to practice.

Scalping Options Trading

This options day trading style refers to the process of buying and selling the same associated asset several times in the same day. This is profitable when there is extreme volatility on the market. The options day trader makes his profit by buying an options position at a lower price and sell it for a higher price. A trader can also sell options position at a higher price and buy it at a lower price depending on whether this is a call or a put option.

This style of options trading is extremely reliant on liquidity. Illiquid options should not be used with this style because the options day trader needs to be able to open and close these types of trades several times for one day. Trading liquid options allow the day trader to gain maximum profitability when entering and to exit trades.

Trading big with this particular style can lead to huge losses in the space of only a few hours. This is why this style is only recommended for disciplined options day traders who are content with seeking small, repeated profits even though it is a less risky method than the others.

It is the shortest form of options day trading because it does not even last the whole day – only a few hours. Day traders who practice this style are known as scalpers. Technical analysis is required to assess the best bets with the price movement of the associated assets.

Pivot Points Options Trading

This option day trading style is particularly useful in the forex market. It describes the act of pivoting or reserving after a support or resistance level has been reached at the market price. It is the same way with support and resistance breakouts.

The typical strategies with this particular options day trading style are:

- To buy the position if the support level is being approached, then placing a stop just below that level.

- To sell the position if the resistance level is being approached, then placing a stop just below that level.

To determine the point of a pivot, the day trader will analyze the highs and lows of the previous day's trading and the closing prices of the previous day. This is calculated with this formula:

(High + Low + Close) / 3 = Pivot Point

The pivot point can also calculate the support and resistance levels. The formulas for the first support and resistance levels are as follows:

(2 x Pivot Point) – High = First Support Level

(2 x Pivot Point) – Low = First Resistance Level

The second is calculated with the following formulas:

Pivot Point – (First Resistance Level – First Support Level) = Second Support Level

Pivot Point + (First Resistance Level – First Support Level) = Second Resistance Level

The options trading range that is most profitable lies when the pivot point is between the first support and resistance levels.

The options day trader is vulnerable to sudden price movements with his style of trading. This can result in serious losses if it is not managed. To limit losses with this strategy, the options day trader can implement stops to marginalize losses. The options day trader can also place two stops, such as placing a physical stop at the most capital that they can afford to part with and another where an exit strategy is implemented.

Chapter Summary

There are three essential components of Options day trading styles:

- Liquidity

- Volatility

- Volume

To take advantage of the options day trading, the trader needs to be very familiar with factors and use them:

Breakout Options Day Trading

Breakout describes the process of entering the market when prices move out of their typical price range.

Momentum Options Day Trading

This options day trading style describes the process of options day trading relying on price volatility and the rate of change of volume.

Reversal Options Day Trading

This style relies on trading against the trend and the opposite of momentum options day trading.

Scalping Options Trading

This options day trading style refers to the process of buying and selling the same associated asset several times in the same day.

This style of options trading is extremely reliant on liquidity

Pivot Points Options Trading

This option day trading style is particularly useful in the forex market. It describes the act of pivoting or reserving after a support or resistance level has been reached at the market price.

CHAPTER 26

Options Trading Strategies

T he following are option trading strategies that should get you trading in no time.

Covered Call Strategy

In this strategy, a trader buys a stock, and then they write a call option for that stock. The strategy generally works well on a stock that the investor is going long on. This means this is not a stock that you wish to speculate, but you would still like to receive some income while keeping it. And if you do sell it, you will sell it at a higher cost.

Here is the strategy in action. Say you own 300 shares of Lemonade Inc. that are currently going at $1.50. Then you write a call option at the strike rate of $1.70 per share, the premium you charge for this is 15¢ per share. If the stock price rises past $1.70 before expiration, let's say it is $1.90, the person you sold the call option will exercise their call option. You will be forced to sell 300 shares at the price of $1.70 per share, but since they will be paying a premium of 15¢ per share, you are selling your shares at $1.85 per share (strike price + premium) which is still high. The 5¢ that is left over is not the money that you lose. It is just money you missed out on. If Lemonade Inc.'s stock price does not rise sufficiently for the call option to be exercised, you will collect on the premium and still keep your shares. Regardless of what happens, you will leave with more money than you started with.

If you aim to keep the stock for a long time, this strategy is good to use, and you don't think the price will increase that much soon but still want to collect some money on that stock. This strategy is also referred to as a buy-write strategy. This even sounds better.

Iron Condor

An iron condor is a complex strategy. It is made to benefit from a small price movement, and it uses four call options. The first two are call options, one of them is long, and one of them is short. The second part is that the long and short options all share the same expiry date and the same underlying asset. You can put this strategy in place with a bearish or bullish. But in principle, the idea is to profit off a little movement.

The Calls

The first call in an iron condor strategy is a sold call closer to the money, while the second one is further out-of-the-money. Just like you would expect in credit call strategy.

The Puts

The first put in the iron condor strategy is a sold put option close to the money, and the second is a bought put option further out-of-the-money.

This allows the trader to cap his losses if he loses the difference between the bought and sold options, just like how it works in a credit call strategy. All options expire worthlessly, and the trader keeps all the premiums credited into his account. The best way to think of this strategy is to think of it as a credit call and credit put strategy. The trade received credit on the upside and the downside.

Straddle Strategy

The straddle is a very profitable strategy used in a market where high volatility is expected. So, you know that the price will move sharply, but you don't know which direction it will go. Regardless, you want to profit from that movement. To profit from an upswing, you buy a call option. To benefit from a fall, you buy a put option for the same asset for the same expiration date at the same strike price. You realize a profit when the money you make is more than the premium you have spent on both options. Now let's return to a Lemonade Inc. example to show this.

Let's say that Lemonade Inc. stock is trading at $100 per share. But you believe because of the pending company announcement, and the price will move sharply in either direction. You buy a call option for a $10 premium per share, and a put option for a $10 premium a share, both at a strike price of $100. You have $10,000 in your account. This will cost you a total of $2,000 in premiums. So, you are left with $8,000. The announcement is made before the expiry date of both options. Lemonade Inc. has experienced losses in the last quarter. Its stock fell by 30%, meaning it is now trading at $70 a share. In this situation, you can buy 100 shares at $70, costing you $7,000 and exercise your put option, selling them for $10,000. You have just made $3,000 on that transaction. You now have $11,000 in your account.

If the announcement made by Lemonade Inc. reports increases in sales and the stock rises by a record of 50%, you will be able to buy 100 shares at $100 and then sell them on the market for $150 each. Since you have $8,000 leftover, you can't afford to exercise your call option. But you use your margin account to borrow $2,000 and buy the shares at $10,000. You make $15,000 on the transaction. You pay your debt, plus interest, and it costs you $2,300. You are left with $12,700. You have made a profit of $4,700.

No matter the direction the stock moves, as long as it is beyond the premium you spent on the options, you made a profit. But if the market price moves only slightly, you will have lost $2,000, and you will be left with $8,000 in your account.

The Strangle

The strangle is similar to the straddle strategy, but instead of buying options that share the same strike price, asset, and expiry date, they buy two options that only share an expiry date and asset. So, the strike prices are different from each other. It is also a strategy often used in situations that are similar to that of a straddle. In both cases, the trader believes that the underlying stock price will move in some direction, but they do not know which. They might have a slight bias about where it might go, but they exercise the strangle to catch profits if they're mistaken. Just like the straddle, if the price does not move enough, the money will be lost on premiums. Time for that lemonade example.

The situation is much like before. Lemonade Inc. will announce, but the rumors around the report are positive, but investors are somewhat skeptical. The stock price is stable, but once the decision is made, the price might move sharply. Thinking the news might be positive, you buy a call option with a strike price at the current stock price. The stock is going at $100 per share. The premium costs you $10 a share. You think it is unlikely that the price will fall, but you want some money for yourself if it falls. You buy a put option at a $98 strike price for $8 a share. You have spent a total of $1,800 on the premiums. Already, this strategy is cheaper than straddle.

Once the stock price falls by 20%, you will collect a profit of $1,800, meaning you break even. If it rises sharply by 50%, you will rake in a profit of $5,000 from the transaction, that minus the premium paid is $3,200. If your bias was correct, you stand to make a few extra bucks

178

that you would miss if using a straddle strategy. If your preference was wrong and the price falls sharply, you would still make money, but you will miss out on some of the action, although this doesn't translate to money lost. In both strategies, the price movement has to be sharp enough to overcome the premium spent. For instance, in a situation where Lemonade Inc.'s announcement doesn't sway the markets either way, and they remain relatively stable, you will have lost $1,800, which is $200 less than you would have in a straddle strategy.

Chapter Summary

Covered Call Strategy

- A trader buys a stock, and then they write a call option for that stock.

- The strategy generally works well on a stock that the investor is going long on.

The Straddle

- The straddle is a very profitable strategy used in a market where high volatility is expected.

- To profit from an upswing, you buy a call option.

- To benefit from a fall, you buy a put option for the same asset for the same expiration date at the same strike price.

- You realize a profit when the money you make is more than the premium you have spent on both options.

The Strangle

- The strangle is similar to the straddle strategy, but instead of buying options that share the same strike price, asset, and expiry date, they buy two options that only share an expiry date and asset.

- The price of the primary stock will move in some direction, but they do not know which.

- Just like the straddle, if the price does not move enough, the money will be lost on premiums.

Iron Condor

- It is made to benefit from a small price movement, and it uses four call options.

- The first two are call options, one of them is long, and one of them is short. The second part is that the long and short options all share the same expiry date and the same underlying asset.

- Like with the strangle, you can put this strategy in place with a particular bearish or bullish.

CHAPTER 27:

Credit Spreads

S preads can be classified in different ways. Credit spreads are distributed strategies that involve total receipts of premiums, while debit spreads include total payments of premiums. It entails promoting a high premium choice while buying a low premium choice in the same category or the same security, which leads to a credit on the trader's account.

The premium got from the written choice is higher than the premium settled for the long choice, leading to a high quality credited into the trader or maybe the investor's account whenever the position is opened. When traders or investors utilize a credit spread program, the maximum revenue they get will be the total premium. The credit spread leads to an income once the options' spreads narrow.

For instance, a trader tools a credit spread program by composing the 1st March call option with a strike price of $30 for $3 plus concurrently purchasing the 1st March call option with $40 for $1. Since the typical multiplier on an equity choice is a hundred, the web premium received is $200 because of the swap. Moreover, the trader is going to profit when the spread tactic narrows.

A bearish trader expects stock prices to reduce, therefore, and buys call choices (long call) in a particular hit cost and offers (short call) the same amount of call options inside the same category and the same expiration in a reduced hit selling price. In comparison, bullish traders expect stock prices to increase, and consequently, purchase call options in a particular hit cost and promote the same amount of call options inside the same category along with the same expiration in a greater hit selling price.

There are different types of credit spreads.

- Bear call spread, which is a beginner-friendly strategy. It employs a bearish outlook that relies on the price of the associated asset decreasing modestly. Profit is gained by finding the difference between the option premium and the commissions paid. Loss occurs when the asset price increases below the strike price.

- Bull put spread is a beginner-friendly strategy with a bearish outlook that relies on decreasing the associated asset price substantially. Profit is gained by finding the difference between the option premium and the commissions paid. Loss occurs when the asset price decreases below the strike price.

- Iron butterfly spread, which involves 4 transactions. The options trader is buying 1 out of the money call option, selling 1 at the money call option, buying 1 out of the money put option, and selling 1 at the money put option, all with the same expiration date and associated asset. This is a complex strategy that is not recommended for beginners.

- Short butter spread, which entails 3 transactions. The transactions are buying 1 out of the money call/put option, selling 1 out of the money call/put option, and buying 1 at the money call/put option with the same expiration date and associated asset. This is also a complex strategy that is not recommended for beginners.

Debit Spreads

A debit spread entails buying a high premium choice while offering a low premium choice in the same category and the same protection, which leads to debit from the trader's account.

Alternatively, a debit spread - usually utilized by beginners to option techniques - requires purchasing an option with a greater premium and concurrently selling an alternative with a reduced premium. The place that the premium settled for the lengthy choice of the spread is much more than the premium gotten from the written choice.

Compared with a credit spread, a debit spread leads to a high quality debited, or maybe given, out of the trader's or perhaps investor's account whenever the position is opened. Debit spreads are largely used to offset the expenses related to owning long features positions.

For instance, a trader buys, one could place a choice with a strike price of $20 for $5 and also instantly sells one could put an option with a strike price of $10for $1. Thus, he paid $4 and $400for the swap. In case the trade is from the money, the max loss of his is lowered to $400, instead of $500.

Different types of debit spreads

- Bear put spread requires 2 transactions and a bearish strategy, which are buying 1 at the money put option and the selling of 1 on the money put option. This is done because the trader is betting that the associated asset's price movement will go down. Profit is earned when the associated asset's price is the same as the strike price of the put option.

- Bull call spread, which is a bullish strategy that includes 2 transactions, which are the buying of 1 at the money call option and the selling of 1 out of the money call option. A trader implements this strategy when he or she thinks that the associated asset's price movement will go up modestly. Profit is gained when the associated asset's price is the same at the strike price of the short call option.

- Butterfly spread, which is a neutral strategy that involves 3 transactions whereby the trader buys 1 in the money call option, sells 2 at the money call option, and buys 1 on the money call option. Profit is gained when the price of the associated asset remained the same on the date of expiration.

- Reverse iron butterfly, which is a volatile strategy that involves 4 transactions. These transactions are selling 1 out of money put option, buying 1 at the money put option, buying 1 at the money call option, and selling 1 out of money call option. Profit is gained when the price of the associated asset falls.

Chapter Summary

A credit spread entails promoting a high premium choice while buying a low premium choice in the same category or the same security, which leads to a credit on the trader's account. There are different types of credit spreads:

- Bear call spread,

- Bull put spread

- Iron butterfly spread

- Short butter spread

A debit spread entails buying a high premium choice while offering a low premium choice in the same category and the same protection, which leads to debit from the trader's account.

There are different types of debit spreads, as well:

- Bear put spread

- Bull call spread

- Butterfly spread

- Reverse iron butterfly

CHAPTER 28:

Rolling Out Options

A rollout is a strategy used to extend the lifetime of an option that hasn't quite worked out. This is going to be a strategy used by options sellers. A rollout might be something you would consider doing when you've sold a naked call, and the share price is closing in on your strike price, creating a risk that the option will be exercised. By doing a rollout, you can keep the trade going longer, and possibly make some changes to give the trade better odds of being profitable. Typically, you will choose to do a rollout when it is close to the expiration date.

A rollout strategy works in the following way. You will close your current option contract by buying it back, and simultaneously open a new contract of the same type, with changes. One way to change is by altering the strike price. Another more common method is to move up the expiration date. A common practice is to open the new contract with an expiration date that is further out in the future. For example, you could close a naked put option that is expiring in two days by buying it back and opening a new contract by selling a new naked put option. You would use the same stock and the same strike price but with an expiration date three weeks into the future. This is a standard strategy where we say that the option contract was rolled out.

You can also follow the same strategy choosing either a higher strike price or a lower strike price. For example, if we have an Apple naked put with a strike price of $205, we could roll up the option by closing this position and selling a new naked put on Apple with a strike price of $206. Alternatively, you could choose a lower strike price. Using the same example, instead of going with a $206 strike price, we could go with a $203 strike price. Maybe, in that case, the Apple share prices are dropping, and it got a little too close for comfort. When you select a lower strike price, they say that you have rolled down the trade.

It's also possible to roll out and roll up or down. You can close your current contract and open a new one that has a further expiration date, but you also change the strike price.

Types of Options Where Rolling Strategies Are Used

You can use a rollout, roll up, or roll down strategy on any option, including options that you buy to open (long calls and puts). However, the vast majority of options contracts that are rolled are short (buy to open) options. You can use rolling techniques on important strategies such as put credit spreads, strangles, or iron condors. The main reason that options traders roll an option contract is that they are in the money, and there is an assignment risk. By rolling it out, you can keep the trade going but avoid assignment. Sometimes just moving the expiration date is good enough to accomplish this. An option can be assigned at any time, but it has to reach expiration to be assigned in most cases. By using a rollout, the trader can avoid this situation. Of course, rolling up or rolling down can also help avoid assignment, since changing the

strike price might allow you to move from an in the money situation to an out of the money situation.

Other reasons are sometimes used to justify rolling an option. For example, when you are selling for income, you can roll the trade to keep generating more money. Changing market conditions might also be a reason to roll a trade.

When rolling a spread, strangle, or iron condor, many possibilities exist for altering the trade. Suppose you have a put credit spread with strikes of $207 and $204. We could change one or both of the strike prices, and we could also change the expiration date. Maybe we want to tighten or widen the spread, roll out and roll down the lower strike price, and have a new spread with strike prices of $207 and $202, for example. It's important to note that a rollout is one trade, and not two. You are simultaneously closing one option (possibly with multiple legs) and opening a new contract.

Chapter Summary

A rollout is a strategy used to extend the lifetime of an option that hasn't quite worked out. It is considered when you've sold a naked call, and the share price is closing in on your strike price, creating a risk that the option will be exercised.

- You will choose to do a rollout when it is close to the expiration date.

- You can also follow the same strategy choosing either a higher strike price or a lower strike price.

- It is possible to roll out and roll up or down.

- You can close your current contract and open a new one with a further expiration date, but you also change the strike price.

Types of Options Where Rolling Strategies Are Used

You can use a rollout, roll up, or roll down strategy on any option, including options that you buy to open (long calls and puts).

- The majority of options contracts that are rolled are short (buy to open) options. By using a rollout, the trader can avoid this situation.

- Rolling up or rolling down can also help avoid assignment since changing the strike price might allow you to move from an in the money situation to an out of the money situation.

- It's important to note that a rollout is one trade, and not two. You are simultaneously closing one option (possibly with multiple legs) and opening a new contract in its place.

CHAPTER 29:

Principles to Success in Options Day Trading

When a trader gets into trading, they are hopeful that everything will play out well and that they will start making a lot of profits in no time. To succeed in trading, a trader must know what trade is all about. This means that they should fully be aware of the strategies in trading, risks involved, how to manage the risks, and, importantly, understand the psychology involved in the trade.

Principle #1 Ensure Good Money Management

Money is the tool that keeps the engine of the financial industry performing in good working order. It is important to learn how you manage your money in a way that works for you instead of against you as an options day trader. It is an intricate part of managing your risk and increasing your profit.

Money management is the process whereby monies are allocated for spending, budgeting, saving, investing, and other processes. Money management is a term that any person with a career in the financial industry, and particularly in the options trading industry, is intimately familiar with because this allocation of funds is the difference between a winning options trader and a struggling options trader.

Money Management Tips for Options Traders

- Define money goals for the short term and the long term to envision what you would like to save, invest, etc. Ensure that these are recorded and easily accessed. Your trading plan will help you define your money goals.

- Develop an accounting system. There are wide ranges of software that can help with this. It does not matter which one you use as long as you can establish records and easily track your money flow.

- Use the position sizing to manage your money and determine how much money will be allocated to entering an options position. To do this effectively, allocated a smart percentage of your investment funds toward individual options.

- Never invest money you cannot afford to lose. Do not let emotion override this principle and cloud your judgment.

195

- Spread your risks by diversifying your portfolio. You diversify your portfolio by spreading your wealth by investing in different areas, add to your investments regularly, being aware of commissions at all times, and knowing when to close a position.

- Develop the day trading styles and strategies that earn you a steady rate of return. Even if you use scalping where the returns are comparatively small, that steady flow of profit can add up big over time.

Principle #2 Risk and Reward Should Be Balanced

To ensure that losses are kept to a minimum and that returns are as great as they can be, options day traders should use the risk/reward ratio to determine each and make adjustments as necessary. The risk/reward ratio is an assessment used to show the profit potential for potential losses. This requires knowing the potential risks and profits associated with an options trade. Potential risks are managed by using a stop-loss order. A stop-loss order is a command that allows you to exit a position in an options trade once a certain price threshold has been reached.

Profit is targeted using an established plan. The potential profit is calculated by finding the difference between the entry price and the target profit.

Another way to manage risks and rewards is by diversifying your portfolio. Always spread your money across different assets, financial sectors, and geographies. Ensure that these different facets of your portfolio are not closely related to each other so that if one goes down, others will not fall. Be smart about protecting and building your wealth.

Principle #3 Develop A Consistent Monthly Options Trading System

The aim of doing options trading is to have an overall winning options trading month. That will not happen if you trade options here and there. You cannot expect to see a huge profit at the end of the month if you only performed 2 or 3 transactions.

You need to have a high options trading frequency to up the chances of coming out winning every month. Develop a system where you perform options trades at least 5 days a week.

To have consistently good months, you need to develop strong daily systems that keep your overall monthly average high. Therefore, creating a daily options trading schedule is key. Here is an example of an efficient options day trading schedule:

- Perform market analysis. This needs to be done before the markets open in the morning. That means that the options day trader needs to get an early start on the day. This entails checking the news to scan for any major events that might affect the markets that day, checking the economic calendar, and assessing other day traders' actions to assess volume and competition.

- Manage your portfolio. The way that an options day trader does this is dependent on the strategies that he or she implements.

Overall, it is about assessing positions that you already have or are contemplating for efficient management of entry and exits. It also allows for good money management.

- Enter new positions. After assessing the market and fine-tuning your portfolio, the next step is to enter new trades that day. Research and efficient decision-making go into this step. The options trader who has already determined how the market was doing and forecasted performance that day would have noticed relevant patterns.

- Incorporate learning during the day. Continual learning is something that an option trader needs to pursue, but this does not always have to be formal classes or courses. You can up your knowledge of options and day trading.

Principle #4 Choose the Right Broker for Your Level of Option Expertise

You have to choose a broker that has an established and long-standing reputation for trading options. You also want to deal with a brokerage firm with great customer service, which can help lay the groundwork for negotiating reduced commissions and allow for flexibility.

There are four essential components that you need to consider when choosing a broker:

- The requirements for opening a cash and margin account.

- The unique services and features that the broker offers.

- The commission fees and other fees charged by the broker.

- The reputation and level of options expertise of the broker.

Broker Cash and Margin Accounts

Every options trader needs to open a cash account and margin account to be able to perform transactions. They are simply tools of the trade. A cash account allows an options day trader to perform transactions via being loaded with cash. Margin accounts facilitate transactions by allowing that to borrow money against the value of security in his or her account. Both of these types of accounts require that a minimum amount be deposited. This can be as few as a few thousand dollars to tens of thousands of dollars, depending on the broker of choice. You need to be aware of the requirements when deliberating, which brokerage firm is right for you.

Broker Services and Features

There are different types of services and features available from different brokerage firms. For example, if an options trader wants to have an individual broker assigned to him or her to handle his or her account personally, he or she will have to look for a full-service broker. In this instance, there minimum account requirements that need to be met. Also, commission fees and other fees are generally higher with these types of brokerage firms. While the fees are higher, this might be better for a beginner trader to have that full service dedicated to their needs and the learning curve.

The advantage to discount brokerage firms is that they tend to have lower commissions and fees. Most internet brokerage firms are discount brokers.

Other features that you need to consider when choosing a brokerage firm include:

- Whether or not the broker streams real-time quotes.

- The speed of execution for claims.

- The availability of bank wire services.

- The availability of monthly statements.

- How confirmations are done, whether written or electronic.

Commissions and Other Fees

Commission fees are paid when an options trader enters and exits positions. Every brokerage firm has its commission fees set up. These are typically developed around the level of account activity and account size of the options trader.

Many brokerage firms charge penalty fees for withdrawing funds and not maintaining minimum account balances—obviously, the existence of fees such as these cuts on any options trader's profit margin. The payment of fees needs to be kept to a minimum to gain maximum income, and as such, an options trader needs to be aware of all fees that exist and how they are applied when operating with a brokerage firm.

Chapter Summary

To succeed in trading, a trader must know what trade all is about.

Principle #1 Ensure

Money management is the process whereby monies are allocated for spending, budgeting, saving, investing, and other processes.

Principle #2 Risk and Reward Should Be Balanced

The risk/reward ratio is an assessment used to show the profit potential for potential losses.

Principle #3 Develop A Consistent Monthly Options Trading System

You need to have a high options trading frequency to up the chances of coming out winning every month. Develop a system where you perform options trades at least 5 days a week.

Principle #4 Choose the Right Broker for Your Level of Option Expertise

Options trading is a complex service, and your brokerage firm needs to provide support when handling difficult transactions.

CHAPTER 30

Options Day Trading Rules for Success

To develop into the options day trader you want to be, being disciplined is necessary. There are options day trading rules that can help you develop that necessary discipline.

Knowing common mistakes helps you avoid many of these mistakes and takes away much of the guesswork. Having rules to abide by helps you avoid these mistakes as well.

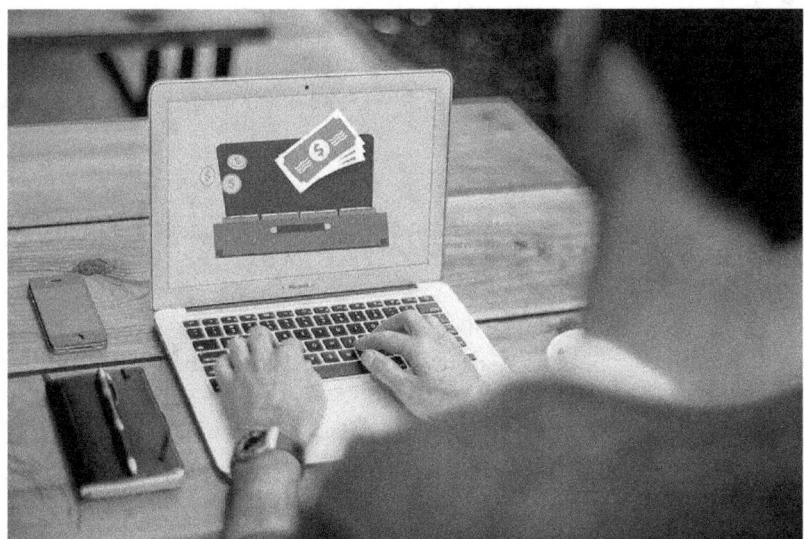

Rule #1 Be mentally, physically and emotionally prepared every day

This is a mentally, physically, and emotionally tasking career, and you need to be able to meet the demands of this career. That means keeping your body, mind, and heart in good health at all times. Ensure that you schedule a time for self-care every day. That can be as simple as taking the time to read for recreation to having elaborate self-care routine carved out in the evenings.

Not keeping your mind, heart, and head in optimum health means that they are more likely to fail you. Signs that you need to buckle up and care for yourself more diligently include being constantly tired, being short-tempered, feeling preoccupied, and being easily distracted.

To ensure you perform your best every day, here a few tasks that you need to perform:

- Get the recommended amount of sleep daily. This is between 7 and 9 hours for an adult.

- Practice a balanced diet. The brain and body need adequate nutrition to work their best. Include fruits, complex carbs, and veggies in this diet and reduce the consumption of processed foods.

- Eat breakfast lunch and dinner every day. Fuel your mind and body with the main meals. Eating a healthy breakfast is especially important because it helps set the tone for the rest of the day.

- Exercise regularly. Being inactive increases your risk of developing chronic diseases like heart disease, certain cancers, and terrible health consequences. Exercise reduces those risks and allows your brain to function better, which is a huge advantage for an options day trader.

Rule #2 Know your limits

You may be tempted to trade as much as possible to develop a winning monthly average, but that strategy will have the opposite effect and land you with a losing average. Remember that every options trader needs careful consideration before that contract is set up. Never overtrade and tie up your investment fund.

Rule #3 Start a small to grow a big portfolio

Start Small to Grow a Big Portfolio

Remember that you are still learning options trading and developing an understanding of the financial market. Do not jump the gun even if you are eager. After you have practiced paper trading, start with smaller options positions, and steadily grow your standing as you get a lay of the options day trading land. This strategy allows you to keep your losses to a minimum and develop a systematic way of entering positions.

Rule#4 Have a realistic expectation

It is sad to say that many people who enter the options trading industry are doing so to make quick money. Options trading is not a get-rich-quick scheme. It is a distinguished career that has made many people rich, but that is only because these people have put in the time, effort, study, and dedication to learning the craft and mastering it. Mastery does not happen overnight, and beginner options day traders need to be prepared for that learning curve and have the courage to stick with day trading options even when it becomes tough.

Losses are also part of the game. No trading style or strategy will guarantee gains all the time. The best options traders have a winning percentage of about 80% and a losing average of approximately 20%. That is why an options day trader needs to be a good money manager and a good risk manager. Be prepared for eventual losses and be prepared to minimize those losses.

Rule#5 Do your homework daily

You need to get knowledge so that you have the basis for making decisions. When you know all there is to know about options, you know what to buy and when to sell, and learn which ones to watch. You are then more comfortable making the right decisions. Always evaluate your choices and see what you have gained or lost so far for taking some steps. Understanding the mistakes, you made guides you to make better decisions in the future.

Rule#6 Analyze your daily performance

To determine if the options day trading style and strategies that you have adopted are working for you, you need to track your performance. At the most basic, this needs to be done because you are trading options daily. It allows you to notice patterns in your profit and loss. This can lead to you determining the why and how of these gains and losses. These determinations lead to fine-tuning your daily processes for maximum returns.

Rule#7- Do not be greedy

This refers to a selfish desire to get more money than you need from a trade. When the desire to get more than you can usually make takes over your decision-making process, you are looking at failure.

Greed is seen to be more detrimental than fear. It places you in a situation where you spend your capital faster than you return it. It pushes you to act when you should not be acting at all.

When you are greedy, you end up acting irrationally. Irrational trading behavior can be overtrading, overleveraging, holding onto trades for too long, or chasing different markets. The more greed you have, the more foolish you act. If you reach a point at which greed takes over from common sense, you are overdoing it.

Rule#8 Pay attention to volatility

Volatility speaks to how likely a price change will occur over a specific amount of time on the financial market. Volatility can work for an options day trader or against the options day trader. It all depends on what the options day trader is trying to accomplish and his or her current position.

Many external factors affect volatility, and such factors include the economic climate, global events, and news reports. Strangles and straddles strategies are great for use in volatile markets.

There are different types of volatility, and they include:

- Price volatility describes how the price of an asset increases or decreases based on the supply and demand of that asset.

- Historical volatility, which is a measure of how an asset has performed over the last 12 months.

- Implied volatility, which is a measure of how an asset will perform in the future.

Rule9# Use the Greeks

Option traders use the Greeks to measure risk in their option positions and their combined positions or portfolios. Greeks are extremely important, and it should be the goal of anyone wanting to trade or invest in options to gain an intuitive understanding. An intuitive understanding of the Greeks will provide you with an understanding of the risk in your option position(s) and greatly contribute to your success as an options trader.

Delta

The Delta represents the amount the value of the option should change with a $1 move (up or down) in the Underlying stock price. Delta means change.

Vega

Vega measures the impact of a 1.00% change in volatility on the theoretical value of an option. It is important to monitor Vega to properly understand the risk in both your long and short positions.

Theta

Theta measures the general daily decay of the option premium, assuming no changes in the stock price and volatility. The life of an option is finite with a defined expiration and, therefore, every day, it decays in value–Theta measures this decay.

Gamma

Gamma simply represents the Delta's change for a given change in the underlying stock–it is the "Delta of the Delta."

Gamma shows the potential for your option position to "move" in terms of value. Note that Gamma can be either positive or negative.

Positive Gamma is generally good for your position, and negative Gamma is generally bad for your position.

Rho

Rho is a measure of the options pricing's sensitivity to a change in the risk-free interest rate. Since interest rates don't change by that much or that often these days, Rho isn't paid much attention to.

Rule#10 Be flexible

Many options day traders find it difficult to try trading styles and strategies they are unfamiliar with. While the saying, "Do not fix it if it is not broken," is quite true, you will never become more effective and efficient in this career if you do not step out of your comfort zone at least once in a while. Stick with want work but allow room for the consideration that there may be better alternatives.

Chapter Summary

Being disciplined is necessary to develop into the options day trader you want to be. There are options day trading rules that can help you develop that necessary discipline.

Rule #1 Be mentally, physically and emotionally prepared every day

Rule #2 Know your limits

Rule #3 Start a small to grow a big portfolio

Rule#4 Have a realistic expectation

Rule#5 Do your homework daily

Rule#6 Analyze your daily performance

Rule#7- Do not be greedy

Rule#8 Pay attention to volatility

There are different types of volatility, and they include:

- Price volatility

- Historical volatility

- Implied volatility

Rule9# Use the Greeks

- Delta

- Vega

- Theta

- Gamma

- Rho

Rule#10 Be flexible

CHAPTER 31:

Common Mistakes to Avoid

There is a lot to learn in options trading as a beginner. It is a world far more complex than trading other securities. A lot is depending on the assumption of the market and the performance of the market in reality. Even the best and most informed guess can and would go wrong. Even the best of the world's traders can't say that they've never been wrong with their assumptions. They don't expect the market to move according to them but change their course of action according to the market.

Starting Without a Plan

Choosing the right option is one of the biggest decisions you will have to make in the trade. Most people don't devote any time to this. If you are planning to do any such thing, then you better donate your capital to charity. It will be put to better work, and you are anyway not going to get anything out of it.

Spend a lot of time in choosing the right stock. Look at the historical movement in the stock. Its performance over short-term and long-term, the volatility in the stock, and the kind of volume it enjoys. All these factors are very important and will play a key role in determining the stock's performance in the market.

Remember that the options contract that you are buying at a specific strike price will have to achieve it within a specific time frame for you to achieve any profit. This is a prediction that will take a lot of hard work.

Assumption of Knowledge

Some people have an assumption that they understand things deeply than others without having any data to prove that. Such people should stay away from options trade. This is a field where knowledge can make a lot of difference, and ignorance can make you lose everything you have.

Options trading is not easy. It is lucrative. It is rewarding. It is anything but easy. The strategies that may not be assuring great returns but will have the lowest risk are the most complex ones. The strategies that offer the highest reward with the lowest capital are the riskiest because they highly expose you to the market risks. You must have a complete understanding of these concepts when you enter the market.

You must understand that all the traders know about the long call and long put options, yet they invest in complex strategies in which they have to invest a lot to get limited returns. They do this because they understand the risk. You will also have to completely understand the risks and trade with strategies that can help you remain secure in the market. You will have to remain consistent if you want to survive in the market for the long-term.

Hesitation to Adopt New Strategies

One thing should be clear in your mind that no strategy is perfect and foolproof. There will be times when a strategy works, and in other scenarios, it won't. You can't remain stuck with one strategy all the time. When you change the trades, the scenarios change with it. You must have the vision to identify the new challenges in front of you and modify your strategy accordingly.

Remember that no strategy is perfect, and you must always remain open to change. No trader should stick to any one strategy for all kinds of situations.

Not Forming an Exit Strategy

Having a good and timely exit plan is a trademark of a good trader. If you see a trade performing poorly and if you still sit with your fingers crossed, hoping against hope for the things to improve, then you can be a great optimist, but you will certainly be a poor or, in fact, a very poor trader.

A good trader will have the foresight to see the implied risk in the trade and the time when the risk increases too much. In case you still have the time to cover some of the losses by squaring off your position, there should be no shame in doing that.

This is an undeniable fact that markets can be very volatile, and the tables might turn at the last moment. In that case, this step can prove to be unwise.

Think of an exit strategy for every trade. Select a point after which staying in that trade would be unreasonable as the chances of recovery of that trade would be extremely low. You must tick that box in your mind and get out of that trade. Later on, even if that trade performs, there is nothing that should worry you as this is not an event that is going to repeat itself very often, but if you don't, you'll see bigger losses very often.

Unreasonable Risk-Appetite

This is another problem with newcomers in options trading. They believe that they have come with the intention of double or nothing. No matter how deep your pockets run but they are bound to get empty very soon if you maintain high risk-appetite.

You must have a reasonable understanding of risk, and you must acknowledge it. You can't keep writing off risks like you are buying lottery tickets and waiting for that once in a lifetime jackpot.

Before you enter a trade, you must evaluate the amount of risk you are ready to take in that strategy. Several strategies limit your risk to a great extent. There is no doubt that they also limit your profit. If you are really into trading, you shouldn't have any problem with a greater number of low paying trades then a fewer number of trades with somewhat higher profit margins and a higher number of loss-making trades.

Not Ready to Take a Beating

As a trader, you can't be adamant. This is a tendency that generally gamblers have. They become more aggressive with every losing trade and keep increasing the bets with the hope that they'll make up for all they've lost in a single trade they win. A trader must think more rationally. Initially, make it a rule to invest a fixed amount in a trade. Even if a trade has gone against you, don't invest more in another trade. Stick with your plan and invest the amount up to which you can take the risk easily. Trading is a very different kind of world. Here, only those people can survive who remain consistent. Even these people take risks, but their risks are always contained. They don't go on a betting spree. They know when to accept defeat and strategize.

Time Frames are Important

This is last but not the least. Time is one of the most important factors in the options trade, as it is decaying fast. All the options contracts come with a predefined expiry. The longer you wait, the faster the degradation would take place in the trade and hence it would be a wise step to keep the time always in sight.

Many traders believe that a trade that's already in profit must be kept till the very end. As a new trader, if the trade is highly volatile, your focus should remain on booking your profit at a reasonable price well with the time limits of the trade. You must understand that near the expiry, the markets can get highly volatile. A trade that might have been looking very lucrative can take a nosedive without much warning, and if you don't have a cover strategy, your loss can be very high.

Always try to focus on a higher number of successful trades. As you gain more experience, your understanding of the market would also improve, and you will be more equipped to take the trades to their deep end. Until you reach that stage, remember that you can only trade as long as you maintain your investment capital and keep building it up.

Chapter Summary

An option trading is more complex than trading other securities. It is a derivative. A lot is depending on the assumption of the market and the performance of the market in reality.

- Starting Without a Plan

- Assumption of Knowledge

- Hesitation to Adopt New Strategies

- Not Forming an Exit Strategy

- Unreasonable Risk-Appetite

- Not Ready to Take a Beating

- Time Frames are Important

CHAPTER 32:

The Platforms and Tools

For you to carry out day trading successfully, there are several tools that you need. Some of these tools are freely available, while others must be purchased. Modern trading is not like the traditional version. This means that you need to get online to access day trading opportunities.

Brokerage

You need the services of a brokerage firm. The work of the firm is to conduct your trades. Some brokers are experienced in day trading than others. You must ensure that you get the right day trading broker who can help you make more profit from your transactions.

Since day trading entails several trades per day, you need a broker that offers lower commission rates.

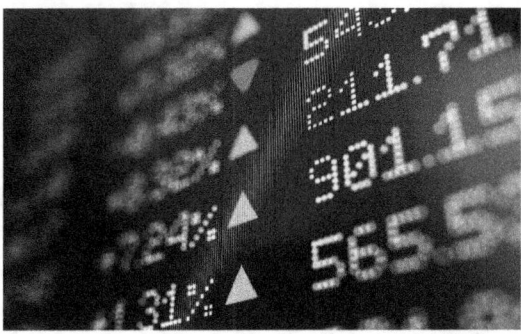

You also need one that provides the best software for your transactions.

If you prefer using specific trading software for your deals, look for a broker that allows you to use it.

Real-time Market Information

Market news and data are essential when it comes to day trading. They provide you with the latest updates on current and anticipated price changes on the market. This information allows you to customize your strategies accordingly. Professional day traders always spend a lot of money seeking this kind of information on news platforms, online forums, or other reliable channels.

Financial data is often generated from price movements of specific stocks and commodities. Most brokers have this information. However, you will need to specify the kind of data you need for your trades. The type of data to get depends on the type of stocks you wish to trade.

Monitors

Most computers have a capability that enables them to connect to more than one monitor. Due to the nature of the day trading business, you need to track market trends, study indicators, follow financial news items, and monitor price-performance simultaneously.

Classes

Although you can engage in day trading without attending any school, you must train some of the strategies you need to succeed in the business. For instance, you may decide to enroll for an online course to acquire the necessary knowledge in the business. You may have all the essential tools in your possession, but if you do not have the right experience, all your efforts may go to waste.

Charting Software

Each of the above charts is created and viewed using specific software. This can be found in a brokerage firm, although you may also purchase this online depending on the type you want to use.

The software helps you identify the right opportunities by indicating when and how you should start and close positions. They always display the necessary patterns required to estimate future changes in stock prices. Using stock patterns, you can also establish continuations as well as reversals in the stock prices.

Chart software is available in many forms. You may find those that are in the form of mobile apps or others that are web-based. Getting the right software enables you to generate correct charts. This explains why you also need to incorporate technical analysis into your trades.

Most day trading chart tools are available free of charge. Some have a forum where you can learn from experienced traders as you use them. They also come with demo accounts that enable you to master day trading techniques before investing in your business capital.

How to Choose Day Trading Charts

Before selecting any charts for your day trading engagements, you must consider several factors. These include:

Responsiveness - This refers to how quickly the chart can display information about the changing market features. This is the first and most important factor you should always check out for. Any delay in the way a chart displays data means that you will not receive vital information in real-time. You may end up acting on old information to make your decisions, which can lead to significant losses on your part.

Most charts may freeze or crash when your computer runs out of memory. This explains why you need a fast processing machine for your day trading business. You want to ensure that the whole process remains as efficient as possible. When testing a chart for responsiveness, wait for a time when the stock market is busy.

For instance, you may try using the chart during a critical financial announcement or news session. If the chart freezes at this point, you will understand that it is not the best one.

Cost – every trader wants to invest in tools that cost less to acquire and maintain. Years back, trading charts used to cost a fortune. This limited the number of traders that could engage in day trading. For instance, traders could buy market data from stock exchanges, and this would also cost a lot of money. Nowadays, all information required for any kind of trading is cheaply available. This means that charts should also not cost as much. There are several alternatives available on the market today for you to select from. As you do this, always have the price in mind.

Stability – a good chart is one that remains online and up to date all the time. For you to succeed as a day trader, you must remain on the market most of the time. If your chart keeps disconnecting from the stock market or fails to display market information on time, then it will make you incur more losses.

You must, therefore, ensure that you remain connected to the market continuously. If you experience instability due to the chart software you are using, feel free to change it. If the instability is resulting from a poor Internet connection, you may need to replace it too.

Type of Indicators – if you have ever engaged in day trading before you understand the importance of technical indicators. Having the right indicators plays a vital role in ensuring you predict the right price movements. Indicators help you to save a lot of capital. They prevent you from making important investments and financial mistakes that may lead to losing your capital.

You may create your indicators, or you may get charting software that has in-built indicators. If you decide to use your indicators, you must ensure that the charting tools you purchase can be used together with these indicators. If not, you might need to stick to those indicators supplied together with your charting software.

Compatibility with your computer – before settling for any charts, check whether it will work well with your current computer resources. This will determine whether you will continue to use your old machine, or if you will have to purchase a new one. Some charts require a lot of RAM space.

If your computer does not have this capability, you will end up adding more RAM. This translates to more yet unnecessary costs. When you are looking around for a chart, ensure that you check how much resources the charts will need.

Most chart packages indicate the minimum requirements you need for the charts to work well. If this is not clearly stated, make sure you ask your provider about it so that you do not make a blind purchase.

User-friendly - a good chart should be easy to use, read, and interpret. A complicated chart will only make your trading days difficult. Get a chart that simplifies the work of interpreting data. Take your time and research on the available options then choose the best in terms of simplicity and layout.

You may consider getting recommendations from other traders, although this does not necessarily mean that the said chart will work for you. Having a complicated chart can make you lose your confidence. You must, therefore, avoid it if you want to have a smooth trading experience

End-user support – once in a while, your chart software may experience a problem that needs technical assistance. As you continue using the software, questions may arise that need the attention of an expert. If the provider is not available to assist or respond to your questions, you may get stuck using the package.

Before making a purchase, ensure that you find the kind of technical support you will receive and how this will be done.

In case you need a highly responsive system, you may need to avoid those platforms that use the support ticket criteria. Companies that use this criterion to solve customer problems always take a long time to respond to even the most critical issues.

Charts play an essential role, and you can use timed and ticked charts for successful day trading. Always remember that different tools are designed for different kinds of trades. You must understand the tools you need as a day trader, so you do not struggle in the market.

Chapter Summary

For you to carry out day trading successfully, there are several tools that you need.

Brokerage

You need the services of a brokerage firm. The work of the firm is to conduct your trades. Some brokers are experienced in day trading than others.

Real-time Market Information

- Market news and data are essential when it comes to day trading.

- This information allows you to customize your strategies accordingly.

Monitors

Most computers have a capability that enables them to connect to more than one monitor.

Classes

You must train some of the strategies you need to succeed in the business.

Charting Software

The software helps you identify the right opportunities by indicating when and how you should start and close positions. They always display the necessary patterns required to estimate future changes in stock prices.

How to Choose Day Trading Charts

- Responsiveness

- Cost

- Stability

- Type of Indicators

- User-friendly

CHAPTER 33:

The Dos and Don'ts of Day Trading

D ay trading is a business that you can set up fast. The very first step is to define if you are a full-time or part-time day trader. The first rule of a trading business is that you should not trade with the money that, if lost, is likely to dent your lifestyle. This money, in the world of trading, is known as 'scarred money.' When you are trading with scarred money, fear comes to haunt your decisions, and you lose more often a winning bet. You will be making the worst possible trading choices and lose money in the end.

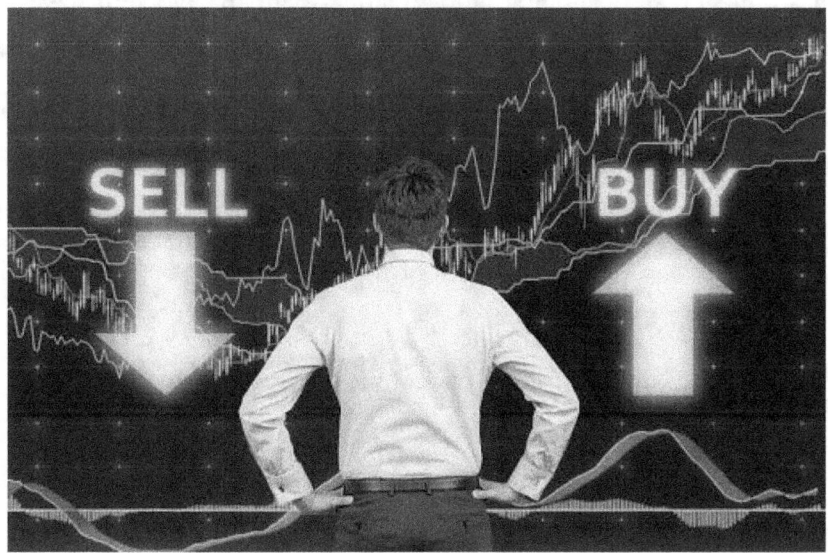

Do's

The basic thing is to be persistent in your approach. You should keep going even amid adversity. No one masters anything from the first attempt. You need time to build and polish your skills. You usually are pretty bad at first, but you learn to make it right over time because you have an urge buried down in your heart to make it better.

Don't try to give up on a couple of failed trades. You may lose some part of your capital while you desperately attempt to bag profits from a trade. If you have failed, you must push past this pain and keep your gaze fixed at the horizon. You must keep in mind the final destination. Only then can you get over the desperation and the frustration.

When you make up your mind about making a career out of day trading, you should create a tangible and practical plan that you must strictly follow. Every business demands a strategic plan that you must build and evolve along the way. A good plan should contain all aspects of your trading strategy. Without a solid plan, you are not trading but gambling. So, don't just gamble. Follow set rules. Your plan may contain the timing of your trade, the amount of initial investment, the companies you want to invest in, the timing you want to hold a stock, and the time you will have to invest in studying technical reports, charts, and volumes of a given stock.

Do prepare a checklist. A checklist usually is as much important as a trading plan. You need to include your trading rules in the list. You should be satisfied with the checklist before you enter a trade. For example, you can decide how much leverage you need to take and the risk-reward ratio. Going through the checklist each time you make a new trade cuts down your chance of making any kind of silly beginner-level mistakes. Once you have done trading for a couple of months, all the checklist points will be fed in your brain, and you will not need them anymore.

You should follow a strict routine. Day trading is not like a job or physical business that binds you for a set period. Trading is a lonely endeavor, and some of you may struggle after finding themselves in a new situation in which they are not under the watch of any kind and are not being instructed on what to do. It is you who have to make decisions and shape your future. Therefore, you must have a routine. It will be risky for your capital and your business if you take long breaks from work during active trading hours. You may miss out on high-probability opportunities. If you have set up a daily routine by defining your goals, you can remain on track and build a successful career as an independent trader.

Don'ts

The very first don'ts of day trading is emotional instability. If you feel that you lose emotional control easily and get angry or overly happy each time you try to make money, you will not follow the recipe to success. A forex trader or stock trader cannot be angry or extremely happy. The best traders across the world are the ones who can part their emotions from trading.

If a person pays heed to rumors around him, the best method to deal with him is to ignore him. You will not like to talk to someone who always lends his ear to rumors about politics or other national issues. The same is true in the world of trading as well. You cannot listen to rumors and act on them.

Remember that you don't need to listen to rumors no matter whatever the scenario is. You must do in-depth research before you act on a rumor.

You should not isolate yourself from others. It is very natural for you to do so because it is the need for this business. There are two reasons as to why isolation happens in the first place. Day traders have to work from home and focus on the latest analysis coming from different sources. The concentration and amount of study involved in its demand that you work in isolation.

Try to focus on teaming up with a group of professional traders who will support each other throughout the busy day. You can sense how other traders are approaching their business and solve the problems that arise over the day.

Chapter Summary

The very first step in day trading is to define if you are a full-time or part-time day trader.

Do's

- Be persistent in your approach.

- Don't try to give up on a couple of failed trades.

- Create a tangible and practical plan that you must strictly follow

- Do prepare a checklist

- Follow a strict routine

Don'ts

- The very first don'ts of day trading is emotional instability

- Do not deal with rumors

- Do not isolate yourself from others

Conclusion

D ay traders involved in the buying and selling of securities are fully investing in this trading activity with multiple learning sources, learning time, and good capital often end up being so successful. Being successful in day trading means acquiring a large portion of profits.

Being a day trader does not come out naturally; a specific personality and traits are duly required. Below are some characteristics of a day trader:

Disciplined

This is a major trait that day traders need to input. Day traders should always be disciplined to remain input when no opportunities emerge and act so fast when opportunities are available. Acting fast also includes strictly considering the step by step rules and obligations initially formed in their big plans.

Open-minded

Day trading is a learning kind of income-generating engagement, implying that there will be happy times and downfalls. Save yourself and learn from all that. Improve the happy times and completely discard the wrong downfall moves. Being exposed to the winnings and failures makes you open-minded, a master of all possible win moves.

A fan of technology

Day trading is carried out in various trading platforms and systems that a trader needs to be familiarized with. This should not scare you. Getting to know how they work does not, in any case, require you to be a computer whiz. Get to learn the basic moves and grow technologically with time.

Mentally tough

Losing market trades are constant; most successful traders will have losing trades every single day. They typically win slightly more times than they lose. Therefore, it is essential to stay focused and rational during a losing period and do not let in the basic fact that money has been lost too. Focus on the future day trading activities by implementing some strategies outlined in a big plan.

Independence

Independence is striving to build the toolbox that will forever lead you. Reading trading books, watching every video, interacting with one mentor after the other, can be a total miss. What if different books have one confusing point on a particular field? What is your YouTube subscriber who decides to quit vlogging? Always grasp the basics after in-depth research and day stay put. Dare to yourself that you've got you and get the large chunks of benefits. However, when you feel you are so lost, do not hesitate to get assistance. Most importantly, master and analyze successful moves and let them be a part of your big plan.

Patience

Good things do take quite some time. In every strategical move, you try to make, think about it carefully, but this should not make you paranoid. Act accordingly with many disciplines to reduce the number of losses likely to be incurred during various day trading activities.

Also, a patient day trader is a learning day trader. Day trading is not going to be easy at first, but with time, when you are equipped with lots of skills and experience, things are expected to flow smoothly. Hey, be patient.

Future-oriented

Getting stuck in the past makes you much of a prisoner. Forward-thinking lets you see the possible moves and gives you the final air when the next trading activity will occur considering the set protocols in the day trader's plan. Being future-oriented incites forward-thinking, which involves rational thinking and knowing your next possible moves after a considerate examination. Being future-oriented hastens and simplifies the day trading operation moves, and the chances are that they will be successful.

Financial freedom

Day trading does not necessarily require you to be a tycoon, but you must have a specific amount of money that has been precisely selected to begin day trading. Remember, first times are always won or lose situations; however, as you continue to learn and grow, this set of money can be lost.

Enthusiasm

High interest in something is a pending successful goal. A great enthusiastic inclination to stocks, securities, commodities, markets, and business gives you the thirst to learn and master what day trading is all about. These are signs of a future successful day trader.

Experience and familiarity

Experience comes with pretty much of downfall lessons and learning. Expose yourself to different learning sources and master every profitable move during day trading to squeeze the best out of that. Getting the trading platforms' experience and familiarity and various strategies needed to be successful at day trading is worthwhile.

Final Word

Thank you for reading! The world of day trading is indeed a challenging one. Day traders are continuously bombarded by news, fundamental market data, rumors, and trading programs that create numerous opportunities. These opportunities are fraught with risk. Given the lightning speed of news delivery via the Internet and the ability to execute trading orders instantly, day trading opportunities are more plentiful than ever.

The risks, as well as the opportunities, demand knowledge, structure, discipline, and profitable methodologies. Key trading tools for success and clear and effective risk management and profit-maximizing strategy form the essential underpinnings of a profitable day trading program. The systems and methods must be put into practice with consistency, organization, and persistence. In short, there is no substitute for practice

There are five key areas to success as a day trader.

Methodology: There are several day-trading methods. The goal is to give a step-by-step procedure by which day trades can be implemented, executed, and managed from the standpoint of risk and reward. The less objective your methods are, the less likely you will be to succeed.

Structure: The essential of all-day trades is a solid structure within which the decision-making process operates. Without a trading model, the odds are that you will lose money, whether you are a day trader or a position trader.

Focus: Most day, traders believe that more is better when it comes to trading. They feel that they must try to take advantage of every price swing or every opportunity that comes their way. In attempting to actualize this feeling, they tend to become scattered in their attention and frequently miss changes in their indicators, or their error rate increases. I believe that in day trading, less is more. It is much better off focusing on a few markets rather than many and a few opportunities rather than many.

Time frame: The time frame in which you operate as a day trader is also critically important. As a day trader, you will be presented with numerous opportunities in numerous of these frames. You need to think and decide if you want to trade in the five-minute, ten-minute, thirty-minute, sixty-minute, or other time frames. Different time frames will give different signals. What may be a buying opportunity in the thirty-minute time frame may be a selling opportunity in the ten-minute time frame. The more time frames you use in your work, the more confused you will become. The one that gets you into a day trade should be the time frame that gets you out of a day trade. Mixing them does not lead to clarity; rather, it is the first step to confusion. Confusion will lead to losses.

Profit-maximizing strategy: You must have and use a profit-maximizing strategy for all of your day trades. Eighty percent to 90 percent of your money will be made on 10 percent to 20 percent of your trades as a day trader. Without the large winning trades, your success as a day trader will be limited. You will generate many small profits, which will be balanced by the cost of commissions and small losses. Unless you have a clear and concise method for maximizing profits, your efforts as a day trader will not be rewarded.

Happy trading!

www.ingramcontent.com/pod-product-compliance
Lightning Source LLC
Chambersburg PA
CBHW070327220526
45467CB00001B/58